Eternally **BAD**

Eternally *BAD*

GODDESSES WITH ATTITUDE

TRINA ROBBINS

Foreword by Rachel Pollack,
author of *The Body of the Goddess*

CONARI PRESS
Berkeley, California

Conari Press books are distributed by Publishers Group West.

Thanks to Ann Forfreedom, for finding and sending me a copy of National Geographic magazine with the information on Dido!

ISBN: 1–57324–550–X

Cover Illustration: Mary Wilshire
Cover Art Direction: Trinia Robbins
Book and Cover Design: Suzanne Albertson
Index: Randall W. Scott
Author Photo: Steve Leialoha

Library of Congress Cataloging–in–Publication Data

Robbins, Trina.
Eternally bad : goddesses with attitude / Trina Robbins.

p.   cm.

Includes bibliographical references.
ISBN 1–57324–550–X (alk. paper)
1. Goddesses—Miscellanea. I. Title.
BF1623.G63 .R63 2001

291.2'114—dc21

2001000516

Printed in the Canada on recycled paper.

01 02 03 TR 10 9 8 7 6 5 4 3 2 1

This book is dedicated to **Blanche** (1991?-2000).

She rose from the streets to become

Blanche the Girl Bandit,

Blanche the Huntress,

Blanche the Bitch Goddess.

Like the women in this book, she is immortal.

Eternally BAD

one
The Evil Twin

Sorceresses: Don't Drink That!

They Got Away with Murder!

by Rachel Pollack, author of *The Body of the Goddess*

Eternally Delightful

What a wonderful book. Trina (rhymes with *Sheena*) Robbins, the eternally young bad grrl of San Francisco, has single-handedly rescued the world's Goddesses from a shadow world of piety and sanctimony. Like one of her beloved woman superheroes (Storyteller Lass?), she has roamed the world of myth and brought back stories that are hilarious, raunchy, and fun.

When the modern Goddess revival began in the 1970s (or the 9970s, as Merlin Stone would say, throwing on an extra 8,000 years to remind us that Goddess culture reaches back a lot further than the "common era"), the very idea of a Goddess religion seemed absurd to many people. Everyone knew that God was a "He." Didn't all the prayers say so? "Our Father, who art in heaven..." wherever that was.

So to get people to take Goddess religion seriously, they had to do two things. First came resurrecting the stories themselves, a massive hunt stretching from Japan to Kenya to Ireland to Navajo Country to Russia. And then they had to express their treasures in a language people raised on Sunday School would recognize as religion. They threw in a few "Beholds," emphasized a universal "Great Goddess" to give things a proper one-God monotheist twist, and they made sure to cut out any parts that were too embarrassing. "The Virgin Mary with crystals," in Trina's great phrase.

As a result, you could read a whole string of accounts of the Sumerian Inanna, learn of her courage as she descended to the Underworld of death, maybe even hear a sanitized account of her voluptuousness or her heroism in defense of her people. But never in any of the books would you learn how much she reveled in war, or how really, really angry she was at her husband for not trying to rescue her, or worst of all (at least in modern eyes) that Inanna was the matron Goddess of touching-yourself-down-there. Or, you could follow the sad tale of Greek Demeter, who lost her daughter to the god of death, without ever learning about Baubo, the old peasant woman who cheered up the Divine Mother by lifting up her skirts for a hot flash that had nothing to do with menopause.

You know something? It's infectious. You read this book and you start thinking, even writing, about Goddesses in a completely different way. As well as bringing back all the naughty bits, Trina has told these stories in a completely new language. Our language. You won't find a "Behold" anywhere in this book, for Trina Robbins knows that the people who first told these stories didn't pitch them in somber high-tone phrases—they spoke in the words of their people. Trina's voice is that of an excited best friend telling you a really hot piece of gossip over coffee and a box of chocolate truffles.

These Goddesses are just like us—or at least us when we don't pretend to be nice girls. They're outrageous, untamed, and dangerous. Just like us. Don't try these stunts at home, Trina reminds us. But definitely read about them. And laugh a lot. And recognize yourself in them. And then give copies of this book to all your friends. Believe me, they'll thank you for it.

This Is Not Your Mother's New Age Goddess!

After being ignored for more than 2,000 years, except when her worshipers were burned to death as witches, the goddess returned to popular culture in the 1970s along with the second-wave feminists, then known as "Women's Libbers." After two millennia, women had grown tired of saying "He" all the time, and found it exhilarating to know that women once had been worshiped as gods. And indeed they had been, as books like Merlin Stone's classic *When God Was a Woman* pointed out, for thousands of years until men took over (don't they always?) and installed deities of their own gender. Even that wasn't too bad at first, when the gods simply joined the goddesses instead of supplanting them, and formed pantheons—entire immortal families with goddess moms and god pops and lots of godly sons and daughters. It didn't get really bad until the men in charge (aren't they always?) decided there was only one deity and he was a He, and anyone who objected should be tortured and killed.

Today, this much is generally agreed upon: Back in the prehistoric, pre-writing days, the earliest people worshiped a female deity. What those early cultures were like is anybody's guess, because darn it, there was no writing. Riane Eisler, in her book *The Chalice and the Blade*, says those were the hunkiest of hunkydory times; women ruled and everybody shared and was nice to each other and sisterhood was powerful. Robert Graves, in *The White Goddess*, writes that ancient tribes used to pick the cutest guy in the village, symbolically marry him to the goddess, and treat him like a king for a year. He slept with all the girls he wanted— and since he was really cute, they wanted him, too—and after the year was up, they'd have a big party during which the women would tear him to bloody bits and devour him. Whom do we believe?

When the new feminists of the '70s brought the goddess back, they were so concerned with being role models that they avoided anything politically incorrect, and that included the darker sides of goddesses, the part that tears guys to bits and eats them. The New Goddesses reflected the New Woman of the 1970s. The goddess became a kind of Virgin Mary with crystals; she was, like, *soooo* spiritual: she was compassionate and healing, and she felt our pain. She was boring.

Bad is somehow so much more interesting than good. Veronica of *Archie* comics is more fun than nice-girl Betty. Pussycats wouldn't be as lovable without their tiny fangs and claws. And honestly now, don't you like the Wicked Queen better than Snow White? From the dawn of time until as recently as 500 years ago, magical and immortal women have been just as bad as they were good, and were often at their best when they were at their worst.

Of course, there is a compassionate and healing aspect to goddesses, and we love them for that too, but there's also a delicious wickedness to be found in stories of goddesses from ancient Sumeria to North America. These immortal bad girls mirrored the faults of mortal women, but on a much grander scale. They loved to party—one of them even invented beer—and just like mortal women, they had terrible tempers. Like mortal women, they sometimes had to cheat and steal in order to get power from men. And while some of them were lesbians who wanted nothing to do with men, others threw themselves away on the wrong guy (and got even when he dumped them!). They stole their sister's boyfriends and husbands—in fact, they were *always* fighting with their siblings—their sex lives were messy, and their bodily functions were even messier. In fact, Grizzly Woman, an immortal Native American ogress, actually had lethal snot!

And we won't even mention the bizarre objects they inserted into themselves for sexual gratification in those pre-vibrator days; you'll have to read about that yourself.

The goddesses—and in some cases, sorceresses—in this book are of necessity from the time when they shared their pantheon with the immortal guys, because that's when people started writing their stories down, but the goddesses were still powerful, and in many cases, more powerful than the gods. No god in Japan was as powerful as Amaterasu, the sun goddess, and in India no god could possibly be as nasty as Kali.

Today we're a trifle more civilized than both gods and mortals were 5,000 years ago. Tearing cute guys to bits and eating them has become passé, although you can still see an echo of it at rock concerts. And this is where the warning, "Don't do this at home" comes in. No matter how obnoxious our brothers may be, we are not savages. We resist the desire to toss the little creep out the window. One doesn't stab one's sister, even when she vamps one's date. And destroying entire villages just because the villagers were mean to your hubby—it simply isn't done anymore.

Still, wouldn't you love to turn that faithless boyfriend into a pig? Because that's what he is! Pissed off about the glass ceiling at work? So were Egyptian goddess Isis and Santería goddess Oya, who resorted to trickery to gain the power they wanted from the men in charge, and Inanna, the Sumerian goddess who got the Top Guy drunk enough so that he gave her his power. Catty friends say you're a slut? Doesn't it feel good to know that one goddess actually slept with a pack of dwarves just to get a diamond necklace, and an Irish queen offered her body to some guy so he'd lend her his prize bull? Or maybe you're a bit of a chunkette, and wear your skirts a little short and tight. Meet Uzume, no extra-small, who took it all off and danced naked in front of 8 million screaming deities.

The point is, There's a little bit of bad goddess in all of us. There's nothing bad we can do that these goddesses, sorceresses, and immortal madwomen didn't do worse, which is why their stories are such fun. Read and enjoy them, find yourself in them (see the quiz at the end of the book), and remember: Nice girls may go to heaven, but badness springs eternal.

one

The Evil Twin

Inanna

Sumer, the earliest known civilization, sprang up around 4000 B.C.E. in the land now known as Iraq. Inanna, the morning and evening star, the mighty queen of heaven, was the ancient Sumerian goddess of love and war, and don't those two things always go together?

One sunny Sumerian morning about 5,000 years ago, Inanna leaned against an apple tree, surveyed her land and herself, and thought about Important Things, as befits a goddess. "Not bad," she commented, looking out upon her fertile fields, and "Girlfriend, you are hot!" she exclaimed, looking down upon her own immortal bod. She was a beauty, Middle Eastern style, from the tips of her gilded toes to her golden breastplates, which were a perfect 36C. Her heavy eyebrows met over her nose centuries before Frida Kahlo made that look famous, and she wore tons of eye makeup.

But something was missing. "Considering that I'm the queen of heaven," she complained, "you'd think I'd have more—well, powers. Like I can't even leap tall buildings with a single bound. Sometimes being a stunner with a perfect body is not enough."

Inanna decided to pay a visit to her grandfather Enki, the god of wisdom. "Grandpa," she told herself, "has lots of powers. Surely he can spare one or two." She ordered her Boat of Heaven brought forth, and had it piled high with beer—lots of beer. Then she sailed down the Tigris to Enki's city, Eridu, situated where the Tigris River meets the Euphrates. In Eridu she found Enki, sitting on a golden throne in his palace built right over the entrance to the Underworld.

Enki looked out over the waters and saw the Boat of Heaven approaching. "Why, it's my granddaughter, Inanna, coming to pay her old granddad a visit," he exclaimed. "I haven't seen her since she was a baby, a mere 5,000 years ago. What a little cutie pie!"

When Inanna undulated off the boat, wiggling her hips a little more than usual, Enki's eyes bugged out, and he repeated, "What a little cutie pie!"

Inanna gave him a granddaughterly peck on the cheek, and said, "I thought we could have a nice visit, Grandpa. I hope you like beer." Meanwhile, her servants unloaded beer from her boat and carried the containers into the palace. By the time they finished, Enki's throne room was filled with huge clay jugs, leaving only just enough room for a table and two chairs, where Enki and Inanna sat down to do some serious drinking. Now, not only was Inanna good at holding her liquor, but when Enki wasn't looking, she poured her beer out into the potted palm behind her. The god of wisdom, however, was a bit of a lush, and as soon as he emptied his bronze goblet, Inanna refilled it like a dutiful granddaughter.

Soon Enki was confiding that Inanna was the best grandchild he ever had, that only she understood him, and that she should have something nice to take back with her. Inanna smiled sweetly and suggested, "Oh Grandpa, I wouldn't dream of asking for anything, but if you really wanted to give me something, a teensy bit of your powers would be nice."

Enki pushed his chair back and stood swaying on his feet. "Done!" he thundered. "I give you the High Priests and the High Throne of Kingship!"

"Ooh, that's nice," said Inanna. "I'll take them." And she refilled his goblet with strong amber brew.

Enki drained the goblet in one gulp, wiped the foam off his mustache, and said, "Plus I give you the secrets of Sex and the Single Girl! I give you everything you wanted to know about sex but were afraid to ask! I give you the temple exotic dancers and the sacred empowered sex workers!"

"That's very sweet of you," said Inanna, refilling his goblet. "Thank you ever so much."

Enki's voice was slurred as he proclaimed, "I also give you the art of song, the art of writing, the art of woodworking and leathermaking and copperworking and goldsmithing."

"Cool," said Inanna, pouring the last of the beer.

Enki laid his head on the table and added, "And I give you the cosmetic secrets of the rich and famous, and the giving of judgments and the making of decisions...." And his voice trailed off.

Inanna politely accepted his gifts and made a decision. She stood up. "Will you look at the time!" she exclaimed. "I simply must run, Grandpa, but thank you so much for all those lovely gifts." And, clapping her hands, she commanded her servants to pile high the Boat of Heaven with all the powers that Enki had given her, while Enki lay with his head on the table, snoring loudly.

The next morning, Enki woke up with a hangover worthy of a god. He groaned as he looked around his empty throne room. "Where are my High Priests?" he demanded, "And what happened to my High Throne of Kingship?"

Enki's servants were afraid to tell him what happened, but his chief servant, Isimud, was braver than the others. He prostrated himself before his king and said, "My king, you gave them away to Inanna."

"What?" roared Enki. "I feel terrible. Bring me some orange juice and send in the temple exotic dancers."

Isimud trembled. "My king," he said, "the orange juice I can do, but I'm afraid you gave your exotic dancers to Inanna yesterday."

"What about my sacred empowered sex workers?"

"Them, too."

"My cosmetic secrets of the rich and famous? The art of song, the art of writing? The giving of judgments, the making of decisions?"

Isimud could only nod.

Enki sat with his head in his hands for a moment. Then he looked up. "How far away is Inanna's Boat of Heaven?" he asked.

"It's on the Tigris River, heading toward Inanna's city of Uruk."

Enki roared, "Don't just stand there! Get the demons of the Underworld, and send them after Inanna before she reaches Uruk! Command them to turn the Boat of Heaven around and return my powers to me!"

So Isimud called forth the demons of the Underworld: hairy, half-animal creatures, giants, and sea-monsters, all to pursue Inanna's boat. Inanna looked back and saw them churning up the foamy water, gaining on her. She called out to them, "Hey, uglies! Quit stalking me! What do you want?"

The leader of the giants grinned, showing off a double row of pointy teeth. "The king wants his gifts back, Inanna," he yelled.

Inanna tossed her long glossy black hair over her shoulders defiantly. She stamped her delicate little golden sandal-clad foot and pouted. "Isn't that just like a man?" she complained. "Promises the moon and then wants it all back. Well, I got these powers from him fair and square, and I'm keeping them." And she called over her own servant, Ninshubur, who was no slouch herself when it came to magic powers. Ninshubur sliced the water with her hand and let out a piercing shriek. A great white wave sprang up and washed all the giants, sea monsters, and animal-men back to Enki's palace in Eridu. Meanwhile, Inanna's Boat of Heaven proceeded on to her city of Uruk, docking right in front of her temple, where she was greeted by a wildly enthusiastic crowd. All of the men were very excited about the temple exotic dancers and the sacred empowered sex workers, while the women were thrilled with the secrets of Sex and the Single Girl, and the cosmetic secrets of the rich and famous.

As for Enki, he sat grumbling in his empty palace. "Young people these days, they have no respect for their elders," he complained. And grandparents everywhere have been saying the same thing ever since.

Inanna, the ancient Sumerian goddess of love and war.

READERS OF THE *Lost Goddesses*

Inanna and her family are the first gods and goddesses whom we know anything about. The ancient Sumerians, who are credited with inventing writing around 3500 B.C.E., recorded their stories on clay tablets. Their dieties were adopted by later cultures with only a change of name. When the Babylonians took over her worship, Inanna became known as Ishtar, but her story remained the same.

There are, however, other goddesses who are just as intriguing as Inanna and her crazed sister, Ereshkigal, but about whom we'll probably never learn. All those fat little goddesses whose statuettes have been found in Europe's caves. Who were they, what were their names and their stories? What high-cholesterol foods did they eat to make them look like that? But alas, the cave dwellers left no records!

What of the beautiful snake goddesses of ancient Crete, with their curls, their heavy makeup, their designer corsets and hourglass figures? Who made their way-cool clothes? Your guess is as good as mine. The lesson we get from all this: Only if it's written down will we remember it. And that's history!

Snake goddess at Knossos

Ereshkigal

Five thousand years ago, the ancient Sumerians neatly pigeonholed their gods and goddesses, giving them each their own domain. While Inanna, the morning and evening star, obviously rules the heavens, there were other gods whose place was the earth, the waters, and even the Great Abyss, which might correspond to outer space. So of course they had a special deity who ruled beneath the ground, in the land of the dead.

The Sumerians were not the most optimistic bunch, as you can tell from their idea of the afterlife. No Happy Hunting Grounds for them, and no Spirits in the Sky, either. Their afterlife was a dismal place beneath the ground where the spirits of the dead moped around with nothing to eat but clay, and nothing to wear but bird feathers, and this depressing place was ruled by Inanna's sister Ereshkigal, the Sumerian queen of the dead.

One day Ereshkigal was in a foul mood. This was not too unusual, as she was often in a foul mood. Ruling the dark, dusty underworld could put anyone in a bad mood. In fact it was so dark that she had a terrible time polishing her long, curving fingernails. She kept smearing the black polish, removing it and starting over. All in all, it was very boring with no one to talk to. The wretched spirits of the dead were too terrified of her to try talking, and the Galla, her scaly demon servants, had long forked tongues and couldn't speak.

To make matters worse, Ereshkigal was having a bad hair day. She was trying to train her hair, or rather, train the snakes that grew on her head instead of hair, to lie in a swoosh across her forehead, but they were not cooperating. Instead the snakes insisted on writhing and hissing in every direction, making her head resemble a pincushion. In a fit of rage, she hurled her polished lapis lazuli mirror at the onyx wall of her palace; it broke into a million pieces. "Oh great!" she exclaimed. "On top of everything else, now I'll have seven years' bad luck."

Just then someone raced into her throne room and threw himself face down before her. It was Neti, the gatekeeper of the underworld, whose job was to open the gate for the spirits of the dead. He was also the only other creature in the place who could carry on a decent conversation. Ereshkigal hardly ever got to see him, because he always sat at the entrance to the land of the dead, up above ground, near the land of the living.

Ereshkigal wanted to ask Neti for news of the aboveground, but before she could open her mouth, he panted, "O great queen, there's a major babe up there, pounding on the gate to the underworld, demanding to be let in. But she isn't dead yet! No one has ever demanded entry to the land of the dead! What should I do?"

Ereshkigal grimaced and bit off a dagger-sharp fingernail. "That could only be my sister Inanna, the queen of heaven and

Inanna at the gates of the Underworld

earth," she muttered, "But what's she doing here, in my domain? She's got some nerve!"

The dark queen looked down at Neti. "Okay, here's my plan," she told him. "Bolt the seven gates of the underworld. Then open each gate just wide enough to let my sister in. But at each gate, strip her of her finery and her power, until you've taken everything away. I'll show her a thing or two!"

And with that, Ereshkigal laughed. Her mad laughter echoed down the endless dark halls of the underworld, and the dead, morosely stuffing clay down their mouths, heard it and shivered.

Neti jogged back to the outer gate of the underworld, bolting all the other gates behind him. He opened the outer gate for Inanna, who waited outside, impatiently tapping her gold painted toes. As she entered, he removed her horned crown.

Inanna reached for her crown. "Hey, wait a minute. Give that back," she cried, but Neti held it up out of her reach.

"You'll have to pay if you want to get into the underworld," he told her.

Inanna shrugged her white shoulders and walked on down the hall till she came to the next gate. But Neti was there ahead of her, and at each gate he took away something else: her beaded collar, her turquoise scepter, her gold breastplate and sandals, her earrings and bracelets, until finally he ripped off her white linen robe, and Inanna entered her sister's throne room naked, humbled, and frightened.

Ereshkigal glared down upon her sister, who trembled before the ebony throne, covered only by her long black hair which hung smooth and shining down to her knees. This sight infuriated the queen of the underworld, who couldn't get her own hair to do anything she wanted. "Mom always liked you better!" she screamed, and hurled a long shard of broken mirror at Inanna. It pierced the goddess' heart, and she crumpled at the foot of the throne, lifeless. (Note: Don't try this at home, no matter how obnoxious your sister gets!) The dark queen clapped her hands three times, summoning the Galla. At her command, they dragged away Inanna's corpse and hung it from a hook upon the palace wall.

Days passed and Ereshkigal remained in a foul mood. Killing her sister had in fact made things worse, because now she felt guilty. She spoke aloud, trying to justify what she had done.

"I'm sort of sorry I killed her. After all, she was my sister. But why did she have to come barging in on me like that? It isn't easy, you know, being queen of the dead. All this has given me a splitting headache."

Of course, nobody answered her. The demons couldn't talk, and the dead were terrified of her.

"Oh, my poor head," she grumbled.

And to her astonishment, two tiny voices spoke in unison, "Oh, your poor head."

At that, Ereshkigal brightened up a bit. She tried, "Oh, my poor stomach."

And darned if the tiny voices didn't answer, "Oh, your poor stomach."

Ereshkigal peered down, and there, standing at the foot of her throne, were two tiny beings. "Oh, my poor heart and liver," she said to them.

"Oh, your poor heart and liver," they answered.

She picked the two little creatures up and held them in the palm of her hand. They stared up at her with big soulful eyes. Ereshkigal was utterly captivated. She didn't know that they were the Kurgurra and the Galatur, created by the great god Enki from the dirt beneath his fingernails, and that he had sent them there to rescue Inanna. In little pouches attached to their belts they carried the water of life and the food of life.

The queen of the dead kissed the Kurgurra and the Galatur on the tops of their tiny heads and murmured, "I like you. Nobody else ever sympathizes with me. You are obviously sensitive and discerning. Let me give you a gift. What would you like?"

"We would like the corpse that hangs from a hook on the wall," they replied.

Ereshkigal yawned. "Oh, that's my sister, Inanna. You can have her if you want, but she's no good anymore, because she's dead."

"Nevertheless," insisted the two creatures in unison, "that's what we want." They sprinkled Inanna with the water of life and the food of life, and she revived.

Ereshkigal was secretly glad that her sister wasn't dead anymore, but she didn't like being outwitted, so she told Inanna, "No one has ever left the land of the dead before. If you wish to leave, you'll have to send someone else back to take your place." And she sent her demon servants, the Galla, to accompany Inanna back to the world of the living, so she wouldn't try any funny business.

On the way back to the earth, Inanna reclaimed her goddess gear, so that she emerged looking as fabulous as when she had left. She went straight to her palace in the city of Uruk, with the Galla following close behind her. As she entered the city gates, she stopped and stared at the sight before her. There sat her husband, Dumuzi, on the queen's throne, wearing the queen's crown upon his head! He was wreathed with flowers, surrounded by dancing girls, and having the time of his life being king now that she was gone. Obviously, he hadn't been mourning his dead wife, nor did he seem to have missed her one bit.

Suddenly Dumuzi saw his wife standing there, her face dark with anger, with the demons behind her, licking their lips in anticipation. Turning pale, he was too frightened to move. The

Galla marched up to his throne and grabbed his arms in their clawed hands.

Trembling with anger, Inanna cried, "Take that no-good bum away!" And the demons dragged the screaming king off to the land of the dead.

All of which put Ereshkigal in a better mood, because Dumuzi happened to be a total stud, even if he *was* a no-good bum.

WHATEVER HAPPENED TO *Dumuzi?*

So did Dumuzi have to stay in the Underworld? Nah, in mythology no one except dead people ever have to stay in the Underworld for good. Eventually Inanna felt sorry for him, especially because his heartbroken sister, Geshtinnanna, petitioned tirelessly for his release. The goddess decided that if Geshtinnanna wanted to save her brother that badly, she could take his place in the Underworld for half the year. Despite his no-goodness, Dumuzi was such a lovable cuss that during the six months he spent underground, even the Earth mourned for him, and all the vegetation died. We call

that winter. Six months later, when he re-emerged, the Earth would burst forth anew with flowers and buds. We call that spring.

Mythology is full of handsome gods and demi-gods, usually the boyfriends of goddesses, who die and are reborn every year. The Babylonian hero Tammuz and the Greek Adonis come back from below every spring, as does Persephone, the only female besides Inanna to return from the land of the dead. Can you think of another well-loved guy who died and came back to life in spring? I knew you could!

Pele and Hiiaka

Before the first American missionaries landed in the Hawaiian islands, in 1820, the Hawaiians had a complicated system of gods, traditions, and taboos. By the time the missionaries arrived, the Hawaiian people were ready to be converted to Christianity, having discarded all their gods except one: Pele, the volcano goddess. When a volcano is that visible, dominating the landscape and always threatening to engulf some unfortunate part of the island with boiling lava, it's not smart to deny the existence of a volcano goddess.

Volcano goddesses are notoriously bitchy, and Pele, the Hawaiian volcano goddess, is the queen bitch of them all. This fiery redhead has a foul temper and a tendency to spew boiling lava at a moment's notice. She is also, however, passionate about affairs of the heart, and the mixture of love and lava is a volatile combination.

Once Pele and her seven sisters, all named Hiiaka, had a beach party at Puna, near her volcano. After a day of swimming and surfing, the goddess decided to nap in the shade of a palm tree, but first she called out to her youngest sister, Hiiaka the Youngest. Hiiaka was as even-tempered as Pele was fierce, and was her favorite.

"Guard me while I sleep, and don't let anyone wake me," Pele told her sister. "I'm going to leave my body and go look for Mister Right. But if I'm still sleeping after nine days, call me back with your magic chant."

So the goddess slept while Hiiaka fanned her gently with a palm leaf. In her sleep, Pele heard the sound of drums. Her spirit rose from her body, left the island of Hawaii, and followed the rhythmic sound all the way to the island of Kauai. There a big bash was taking place at the palace of Lohiau, chief of the island. Pele, who could look however she liked, took on the form of a knockout hula girl and ambled into the feasting hall. The drums stopped and everyone turned to stare at the gorgeous creature who approached the dais where the king sat. Lohiau was a really cute beach boy–type. "That's my future squeeze, my sweetie, the man for me," said Pele to herself, and, with a smile and wink at the king, she seated herself at the foot of his throne.

"Where are you from?" asked Lohiau.

Pele blinked her long lashes at him coyly. "Oh, here and there," she murmured.

Now, there were three others at that feast who, like Pele, were no ordinary women. They were actually mo'o, fearsome dragon sisters disguised as sultry crimson-lipped femmes fatales. They had come to the feast because their oldest sister, Kilinoe, had a major crush on Lohiau. Kilinoe knew hard competition when she saw it, but she wasn't about to give Lohiau up to Pele that easily. Slowly and languorously she rose, clapping three times to the drummers.

Then, never taking her eyes off the king, Kilinoe performed a killer hula. As she swayed her hips in rhythm to the drums, Lohiau tried hard to keep his eyes on her hands. There was no denying Kilinoe was a hot dancer, but the volcano goddess upped the ante. As soon as Kilinoe finished her hula, Pele stood up. The drummers started up again, but Pele held up a hand to silence them.

"Forget it," she said. "I don't do drums. I dance to the wind!"

Warm breezes filled the hall, and Pele started a slow, gentle hula. Then she quickened her steps and the breeze became a chill wind. Her dance grew fiercer, and outside the palms bent to a hurricane, while white waves formed on the sea. The guests shivered and drew their feathered cloaks closely about themselves.

Pele, the Hawaiian volcano goddess

Kilinoe and her sisters stomped out of the hall in a snit. They knew when they were licked.

Pele ended her hula and the winds faded away, leaving the guests to wonder if they had imagined the whole thing. When she took the empty seat next to the king, nobody objected. As for Lohiau, before the party was over, he proposed to Pele and she accepted. But nine days later, she heard her sister calling her back.

"It's been fun, and I hate to leave, but I'm afraid I have to go now," she told her new husband. "I promise to send for you soon, so wait for me and be good." Then, before his astonished eyes, she disappeared.

Pele awoke in her own body, on the beach at Puna, and was so happy to be back with her sisters that she forgot all about Lohiau. It was days before she remembered that she'd left a husband back on Kauai. She sent a message to her kid sister at the lehua groves where she made her home. Hiiaka preferred the scarlet blossoms in her perfumed gardens to the smoky volcano, but when she got the message, she sped to her sister's side.

When Hiiaka arrived at the volcano, Pele told her the whole story. "Remember that long nap I took? Well, I left my body and met the cutest guy, and I married him. Now I need you to go to Kauai and bring him back to me. Just remember, he's mine."

Hiiaka said, "Yeah, right. And the minute I turn my back, poof! Flaming lava all over my lehua trees. I know you."

"No really, I'll be good, " protested Pele. "As long as you keep your hands off my hubby."

So Hiiaka set off on her way to Kauai. It wasn't easy going though, because there were monsters living on the land and eating unwary travelers for brunch. Hiiaka, being a goddess, destroyed the monsters she met along the way, making the land safe for everyone else. Finally she arrived in Kauai, only to be greeted with sad news. After Pele left him, the king had died of a broken heart. To make matters worse, the dragon sisters had stolen his body and dragged it up to their dank, watery cave high on a cliff, where Kilinoe, the oldest sister, jealously guarded it. "I couldn't have you when you were alive," she told the dead body, "but now you're mine!"

Hiiaka was too perky to let a small setback like this get to her. She scaled the cliff, chanted one of her magic chants at the dragon sisters, and reduced them to a harmless mist. Then she searched out and found Lohiau's soul resting in a niche in the rocks, where it had been tenderly placed by a moonbeam. She put the soul back into Lohiau's body, and he returned to life. A rainbow formed from the mouth of the cave to the ground below, and Hiiaka and Lohiau descended, hand in hand. The people of Kauai, always ready to party, wanted to celebrate their king's return, but Hiiaka, who knew her sister well enough, told them there was no time to celebrate. If they didn't return soon,

Pele would grow impatient and jealous. If only she knew how true her predictions were!

So Lohiau left his land under the rule of his best friend, Paoa, and, along with the young goddess, headed for the big island of Hawaii. It took them quite a long time to get back, but all that time, even though the prince was a total stud, Hiiaka respected her sister's wishes and kept her hands to herself.

Meanwhile, back at the volcano, Pele, who was not the most patient of goddesses, seethed with jealous rage. She sat alone in her fire pit, bathed in flames, muttering to herself. Her sisters had long ago learned to avoid her when she got that way.

"At this very moment, they're probably making out," she snarled. "Making out, hell! I bet they're doing it! I should never have sent Hiiaka, she's too young and pretty! I'll get even with her." And in a fit of insane paranoia, she covered Hiiaka's beloved lehua groves in flaming lava. "Steal my husband, will she? That'll show her!"

At that moment, Hiiaka and Lohiau had finally reached Hawaii, and the young goddess stopped on a high mountain peak to look over the land. There in the distance were the smoldering remains of what had been her favorite gardens. After all she'd gone through to return her sister's husband! "That does it," Hiiaka exclaimed. "No more nice gal." Standing on the rim of the crater in full view of her sister, she gave Lohiau a big

Pele, the Hawaiian volcano goddess

smooch. To make matters worse, Lohiau, getting over his surprise quickly, kissed her back.

Pele was so furious, she sent her sisters out to burn him up, but he was so handsome that they couldn't bring themselves to obey. "Bah!" she exclaimed. "If you want something done right, you always have to do it yourself!" Running up the hill in the form of molten lava, she threw her arms around Lohiau, turning him into a tall stone.

Months went by. Back in Kauai, Paoa decided to go to the Big Island and find out what had happened to his friend. Arriving at the volcano, he found Pele sitting with her sisters. The sisters were all beautiful hula girls, with blossoms in their long raven hair and leis around their slim necks, but Pele had taken the shape of an ancient hag, blackened and sooty.

Paoa declared, "I know one of you is Pele. Let's see if I can find the right one."

He took each goddess by the hand. Their hands were soft and warm. Then he took the hand of the ancient crone, and it burned him like the fires from the volcano. He knelt before her. "This is Pele."

Pele was pleased, and she became a beautiful young woman again. Paoa, she thought, was pretty cute, too. In fact, he was cuter than Lohiau. He asked the goddess what had become of his friend.

"Oh, I got mad at him, so I turned him into that rock over there." Pele yawned, gesturing toward the crater's rim.

Paoa was horrified. "What? After Lohiau died of love for you, and Hiiaka brought him back to life, you did that?"

Pele looked over to a corner of the pit where her sister slumped listlessly. "Is that true?" she demanded. "Did you really bring Lohiau back to life for me?"

Hiiaka pouted. "Yes, I did, and I must say you weren't very grateful."

"But why didn't you tell me?" asked the fire goddess.

"Like you really gave me a chance," sniffed her kid sister.

"That changes everything," declared Pele, and she brought Lohiau back to life. "You can have him, " she told her sister. "Anyway, you deserve him." Actually, she had lost interest in Lohiau. She liked his friend much better.

Hiiaka went back to Kauai with Lohiau and lived happily with him for the rest of his life. Then she returned to her sisters in the volcano. As for Pele, she probably eventually grew tired of Paoa, but the story doesn't tell whether or not she turned him into stone. Whatever happened, it's not particularly lucky to be the object of Pele's passion!

THE GODDESS WITH A *Sense of Humor*

Pele's latest eruption, which has been flowing continuously since 1982, does have its amusing moments. Unlike Vesuvius, which utterly destroyed and obliterated the ancient Roman city of Pompeii before anyone had a chance to escape, Pele's flow has been so slow and comparatively gentle that residents of the Big Island are given plenty of advance warning that their homes are in the direct path of the eruption. Thus, we get the spectacle of people, having moved out all their precious possessions, parked safely across the street on lawn chairs, sipping ice-cold beer as they watch their houses consumed by molten lava.

Namaka O Kahai

Back in the misty past, before the deities came to Hawaii, legend has it that they lived on a mystic island with the jaw-breaking name of Kalakeenuiakane. Two members of this Polynesian pantheon were the sisters Pele and Namaka O Kahai, who were as different as fire and water—literally, as Pele was the fire goddess and Namaka was goddess of the sea—but it would be hard to say which of them had a worse temper. Now, Namaka had a really cute surfer-boy husband named Aukele Nui A Iku. That's Hawaiian for "to swim" and "to glide," so we know he was a surfer! Although Namaka was a lovely ukulele lady herself, she was jealous of her gorgeous kid sister, and as far as babes were concerned, she didn't trust

Aukele as far as she could throw him. Not a particularly good way to start one's marriage. So she simply never mentioned to her new husband that she had any sisters, and she didn't invite Pele, or any member of her family, to the wedding. Actually, Namaka had eight sisters, all stunners: Pele and seven other goddesses, all named Hiiaka. Who knows why, maybe their parents had run out of names. But Namaka was most jealous of Pele, whose beauty burned bright as a flame.

Kalakeenuiakane was a small island, and you can't keep sisters hidden for long on a small island. One day when the surf was up, Aukele took his board and headed for the best beach on the island. There, sunning herself on a rock, twining flowers into her long fiery hair, sat the ultimate hula girl. Aukele's mouth dropped open and his surfboard fell to the ground. Pele smoothed her low-cut sarong and smiled at the astonished beach boy. "Aloha, brudda," she said. "Cat got your tongue?"

Before you could say, "Hang ten," the two were side by side on the warm sands, copying that scene in *From Here to Eternity*, with Pele teaching Aukele some hula moves he'd never known before. That, of course, was when Namaka showed up. "My husband!"

she shrieked. "And my sister!"

Pele sat up and adjusted her sarong. "Your husband?" she echoed. "You're kidding!"

Aukele scrambled to his feet. "It's not what you think, dear," he ventured.

Namaka's blood boiled in her veins like an angry ocean. "I'll deal with you later," she yelled, shoving her husband out of the way and descending on her sister. What happened next was a worse catfight than anything you've ever seen on Jerry Springer. It went far beyond mere hair-pulling. Namaka went for the throat—she was actually trying to kill her sister!

Pele managed to break away and sped like a runaway fire to the other side of the island, where her sisters lived.

Namaka O Kahai, the Hawaiian goddess of the sea

"Quick!" she gasped. "Namaka's after me! We gotta get away!"

Pele and all the Hiiakas piled into a boat and paddled furiously, managing to stay just ahead of the giant waves that Namaka sent after them. They rowed north until the mountains of Kauai rose up in the distance. Hiiaka One saw them first through her spyglass and yelled, "Land ahead!"

"And about time, too," muttered Hiiaka Two. "All this heavy rowing is ruining my manicure."

"Faster!" called out Hiiaka Three. "She's gaining on us!"

All the Hiiakas rowed as though their lives depended on it, which they did. As soon as their rowboat touched the beach, Pele leaped out and looked for a place to dig with her digging stick. Being a volcano goddess, she needed fire in order to survive. "Must...have...fire..." she panted, digging with all her might, until she had opened a volcanic crater. She eased herself into the good bubbling lava and heaved a sigh of relief.

But Namaka was not that easily beaten. She sent a tsunami that flooded Pele's new home and quenched the fires. The eight sisters packed their ukuleles and sarongs and moved to Oahu, where Pele dug another, bigger firepit at Diamond Head. Then, while Pele took a beauty bath in her restful flames, the Hiiakas all went down to Waikiki and checked out the surfing scene.

Ah, but the smoke rising from Diamond Head betrayed Pele's new address to Namaka, and she sent another tsunami to douse her sister's fires. Once more the sisters had to pack up their meager belongings and move, this time to Maui. All this moving was starting to wear on the faithful Hiiakas, who especially hated to leave Waikiki, which had such a good beach.

One day, Namaka, watching from the highest spot in Kalakeenuiakane, saw smoke rising from Haleakala on Maui, and she knew what that meant. She gnashed her teeth angrily. "It's that tramp, that husband-stealer," she muttered, "Thinks she's escaped me, does she? I'll show her!" And she rode a single enormous wave from Kalakeenuiakane right up to Haleakala, where she confronted Pele, who had actually started believing she was safe. All the ruddy color drained from Pele's face, and she backed up to the wall of her firepit. "Can't we discuss this in a civilized manner?" she asked her sister.

"Hah!" sneered Namaka, "This is a fight to the death! Only one of us is gonna leave this pit alive!" She had a razor blade hidden in her hair and intended to cut Pele into bite-sized chunks. The battle that ensued lasted for months! Pele, hardly a wuss herself, put up a good fight. She tried defending herself with fire, but Namaka's water kept putting out the flames. The Hiiakas screamed and covered their ears. They ran and hid on the other side of the island.

Finally, the thunderous yells and bloodcurdling shrieks ended. The Hiiakas stared at each other for a moment, then ran back to Haleakala, where they were met by a dreadful sight. Bones were strewn all along the shore, and over the bones stood Namaka, brushing the dust off her hands. Without even a glance at her horrified sisters, the sea goddess dove into the water and swam away, leaving the Hiiakas alone and miserable. They were too depressed to even bury their sister, and to this day the masses of broken lava beneath Haleakala are called Naiwi O Pele, the bones of Pele.

For a long time Pele's sisters hung out at the beach, playing sad songs on their ukuleles and seeking forgetfulness in tall fruity drinks decorated with tiny paper parasols. Then one day, Hiiaka Seven chanced to look across the water at the Big Island of Hawaii, and there, in the middle of the island, she saw smoke and flames rising from Kilauea. Pele was back in town! It simply is not that easy to kill a goddess.

The Hiiakas skipped merrily over to the Big Island, where their big sister awaited them in the firepit of Kilauea, which she had decorated cozily with rattan furniture, bamboo-framed menus from ocean cruises, and cushions in a tropical print, and there they live to this day. As for Namaka, ignorance was bliss. Convinced that she had done in her sister, she forgave her erring beach boy and they lived happily together. Then one day she happened to glance toward Hawaii and saw a great column of smoke arising from Pele's new home. But by now she'd gotten all of that rage out of her system, so she just grumbled, "Sisters! Who cares?" and went about her business. Perhaps one reason she wasn't angry anymore was because she knew what would happen in about a million years, which isn't very long by goddess standards. Namaka's pounding surf is constantly washing away bits and pieces of Hawaii, and one day the islands will be completely worn away. Namaka will have won at last.

Of course, Pele knows this too, and that may be one reason for her terrible temper.

ALL THOSE *Hawaiian Dieties*

Hawaii, when Captain Cooke landed his ships on the island, was a tangle of rules and religions. The Hawaiians had *too many* gods and goddesses, and a complicated system of taboos, most of which had women on the losing end. For one thing, women were forbidden from eating with men. Among the foods they couldn't eat, under penalty of death, were bananas, coconuts, pork, and that special Hawaiian delicacy, baked dog. The poor things must have lived on

Hawaiian deities

fish, which by the way, they were not allowed to catch. On the positive side, men had to do all the cooking.

Queen Kaahumanu, the favorite wife of King Kamehameha and Hawaii's first feminist, changed everything. When her husband died, she put on his feathered cloak, took up his spear, and became Kahuna Nui, or joint ruler of the islands, along with the new king Liholiho, Kamehameha's son by another wife. Kaahumanu and Liholiho's mother felt humiliated by the taboos forced upon them, and worked together to change the situation. They started by openly eating bananas in front of the young king, and by the time they were through, he had joined the women at their eating table.

The Hawaiian people were shocked, then delighted. They hated their elaborate system of rules and taboos, and embarked on an enthusiastic orgy of destruction of their idols and temples. Then, just when they had tossed the last of their wooden gods into the bonfire, who should show up but the missionaries, with their own set of elaborate rules! Ah well, easy come, easy go.

two

Tramps and Thieves

Freya

Norway, Sweden, Denmark, and Iceland, the homes of the ancient Vikings, are as far north as anyone would want to be, and the Viking's myths were filled with ice images: vast worlds of ice inhabited by frost giants with ice for hearts. On the other hand, Asgard, the home of the Vikings' gods, was always warm. The Vikings were a brawny, brawling lot, and their pantheon of gods resembled themselves. Big, bearded Odin was the father of a feuding, fighting family: mighty Thor, whose hammer made thunder, the trickster Loki, whose idea of a good joke was to kill his brother, and several big-boned goddesses with braided hair and horned helmets, who were as tough as the gods. The most beautiful of these was the golden-haired Freya, the Norse goddess of love.

Freya had everything a girl could want: a fabulous figure, a gorgeous wardrobe that included a golden bustier, and some of the best methods of transportation in the ancient world. She traveled around the sky in a cart pulled by two giant cats. When she rode at the head of the Valkyries, her own band of warrior maidens, she and they flew through the air on great white winged horses, scooping up dead Viking heroes on the battlefield, taking them over the rainbow bridge to Asgard. Because the Vikings liked to fight so much, this scooping up process was a daily occurrence.

Freya, the Norse goddess

Most of these heroes wound up at Valhalla, Odin's palace, but Freya chose the cutest of the dead guys for her own castle in the clouds, Folkvand. There they spent eternity in her great hall, drinking mead from golden horns, drunkenly singing war songs and boasting of their bravery. These war heroes were not particularly bright, but they had great muscles and long, braided, fair hair, and Freya, being the goddess of love, often picked the least drunken of the bunch to share her great canopied bed and bearskin comforter at night.

There was only one thing missing in Freya's life, and that was a fabled diamond necklace called the Brisingamen, which was supposed to be the most beautiful necklace in the whole world. She'd never actually seen the Brisingamen, because it was owned by dwarves who lived deep inside the Earth, but she wanted it badly.

Freya became obsessed with the Brisingamen. Each night she would sit at her dressing table, trying on jewelry in the mirror. Holding up a brilliant necklace, she would sigh, "It's not bright enough for my white neck. There is only one necklace which could be bright enough for my neck." And she would toss it aside.

Finally she made a decision "If the Brisingamen won't come to me," she vowed, "I must go to the Brisingamen."

She braided her golden hair into two long braids that reached to her knees, threw a gray cloak over her gold bustier, took up a stout oak walking stick, and left Folkvand without looking back.

Over the rainbow bridge that sepa-
rated Asgard from Earth she
marched, wearing dainty embroidered slippers. Into a hole in the west
of the Earth she went, down through
the darkness. It was cold and damp
beneath the ground, but Freya carried her warmth within her and pro-
vided her own glow as she ventured
into tunnels where creatures lived
that had never seen the sun.

Finally, in the blackness Freya
saw a faint light, which grew
brighter as she approached. She
turned a corner and found herself at
the mouth of a great cavern in the
heart of the Earth. The glowing
walls were veined with gold and
precious stones. Little men, gnarled
and brown as the roots of trees, dug
out the treasure with tiny pickaxes.

Others forged shining weapons over white-hot fires, while still
others sat at benches with tiny hammers, crafting magnificent
brooches, rings, and even royal crowns. Floating in the air high

above all, illuminating the cavern as the sun lights the Earth, hung the fabled Brisingamen.

Freya caught her breath. Everything she had heard about the necklace was true. It was crafted from purest gold, and set with perfect, *enormous* diamonds! She reached up for it—and yet it floated higher, just out of her reach.

The dwarves stopped what they were doing and turned to look. "Well, well, we have a visitor," said one. Their voices were hoarse and rusty, as though they didn't speak very often. "Ooh, she's pretty," said another. "She shines," murmured a third. "I bet she's the goddess Freya."

Freya introduced herself. "I've come for your necklace, the Brisingamen. Don't you think it's wasting away down here in the dark, when it should be shining around my white neck?" She reached up for it, but again it floated away, just out of her reach. "I seem to be having a hard time catching it," she declared. "Will you please help me?"

The dwarves laughed their hoarse, rusty laugh. "The Brisingamen will come only when we call it. If we give you the Brisingamen, what will you give us in return?"

"I'll let you have my bravest, handsomest warriors."

The dwarves laughed again. "What do we want with warriors? Can they craft fine jewelry? They're clumsy; they'll just get in the way."

"Well then, I'm an earth goddess. I can send you flowers and fruits from the land above your heads."

"Flowers will wither and die in the darkness. Fruits will rot."

Freya grew desperate. She had to have that necklace! "Tell me what you want."

The little men all cried out together, "You! We want you! You're a major babe!" They leered at her. "Come live with us, and we mean live with us, if you know what we mean, and we think you do."

Freya knew what they meant. She looked at them. They were covered with soil and pebbles and they were ugly as toads. Then she looked up at the Brisingamen, glittering from the cavern's roof. She looked back at the dwarves and back at the Brisingamen. Finally she sighed.

"Okay. But you all have to take baths."

The little men grumbled, but they took baths. And once they were scrubbed clean, Freya decided that, after all, toads aren't really so ugly. In fact, she thought, the little guys were kind of cute.

So Freya slept with a different dwarf each night, and boy, were they grateful. They fed her gourmet food in golden dishes and dark wine in crystal goblets. They sang songs about her beauty, showered her with rubies and emeralds, and then finally one day, one of the dwarves stretched out his hand and the Brisingamen floated slowly down until it rested in his callused palm. Freya knelt, and the dwarf fastened the glittering necklace around her neck. He looked a little sad, but he said, "A bargain is a bargain."

Freya hugged all the dwarves good-bye—she had grown quite fond of them—and ascended back to her castle in Asgard, and to her husband. Did I mention that she had a husband? Well, she did, though you'd never know it by her behavior. His name was Odur, and he was god of the sun, but when Freya opened the door of her castle, calling, "Honey, I'm home!" the house was empty. Odur had left a note:

Freya, you tramp!

The war heroes I could handle. After all, they are brave and hunky, and if I liked boys, I might be tempted myself. But the dwarves are another story! Did you really think I wouldn't find out? This is the last straw, and I'm leaving. Have a good life.

Your broken-hearted husband,
Odur

Freya sobbed into her delicate lace hanky, because Odur had been a good husband, and extremely understanding, and now he was gone. Then she spotted herself in the mirror, with the magnificent necklace glittering around her neck. She wiped her eyes and smiled at her reflection. "Who cares?" she told herself. "Husbands may come and go, but a diamond is forever."

FROM *Naughty to Nice* IN 2,000 YEARS

In case you hadn't guessed, the tale of a fair maiden living with little men was repeated through the centuries, until a much cleaned-up version was finally written down by the Brothers Grimm, and called *Snow White and the Seven Dwarves.*

Snow White and the Seven Dwarfs

Isis

Isis wasn't always the supreme and beautiful winged goddess of ancient Egypt. Once she was as mortal as you and I, and at one time happened to be the greatest magician in the known world. In those days all the power belonged to Ra, the sun god, known to everyone who has ever done a crossword puzzle.

This was an incredibly ancient time, way before the pyramids were even a gleam in Pharaoh's eye, and Ra, who had been a god since the dawn of time, definitely looked his age. There was no spot on his leathery face that wasn't wrinkled, and he walked stooped over, with the halting pace of a gazillion-year-old god. Mortals were not allowed in the sun god's domain, but one day Isis watched from a safe distance as he shuffled through his celestial garden, leaning on a solid gold walker. Her lip curled in disgust.

"Jeez," she told herself, "this is really pathetic. That geezer has divine powers while I, young and beautiful, and with a really high I.Q., must remain mortal. Oh, gross! Now he's dribbling down his chin!"

Then as she watched the old god's spittle drip from his chin onto the dirt path, she got a brilliant idea. Waiting until the immortal duffer had passed, she sneaked up to where his divine, though disgusting, saliva lay puddled in the dirt. Mixing up a mud pie of saliva and dirt, she brought it home and shaped the mud into a snake, muttering incantations over it. Soon the wet brown thing began to wriggle and hiss; it had become a small but deadly snake.

Isis

Isis fed the snake a mouse to keep up its strength, and put it into a cage. The next day, holding it gingerly by the tail, and keeping it away from her body, she tiptoed back to Ra's garden. When the old god wasn't looking, she deposited it on the path where he walked. Then she hid behind a patch of papyrus and waited.

The approaching radiance signaled that Ra was on his way. "For an old god, he still shines brightly," she thought, putting on her sunglasses. The ancient sun god came trudging along in golden sandals, muttering to himself, "Am I not the Ancient and Most Powerful One? Am I not Radiant and All-Knowing?"

But of course he was not all-knowing, or he would have known that a magic snake lay in his path. "Ouch!" he exclaimed, as it bit him on the heel. He picked the snake up by its tail and dashed it against a rock, but it had already done what it was created for. "That hurts," he muttered, hobbling down the path. "That really hurts!"

Satisfied that her plan was working, Isis took off her sunglasses and went home. "So far, so good," she said.

Ra lay in bed in his celestial palace, writhing in agony. Because he was immortal, the snake's deadly poison couldn't kill him, but it hurt like the dickens. Plus, he was confounded. "How is this possible?" he moaned. "None of my creations can hurt me, and I created *everything!*" But of course it was Isis who had created the snake.

A long line of divine physicians, sorcerers, and magicians filed into Ra's bedroom. They had the heads of cats, hippopotamuses, cranes, and ibises. They took his pulse, looked at his tongue, listened to his heart, and shook their various animal heads. One prescribed a concoction of adders' tongues boiled in wine, another suggested bleeding him, a third applied leeches. Nothing worked. The sun god raged. "What good is being immortal if I must suffer through eternity? Is there no one who can help me?"

A minor jackal-headed doctor spoke up. "O, all-powerful one, there is somebody. I've heard that she is the greatest magician on earth. But she is a mortal."

The other gods were shocked. "A *mortal?* How can a mere mortal cure a god?"

The jackal-headed god persevered. "She's really, really good. I know someone who knows someone who said she cured his brother. And his brother was already *dead.*"

Ra was desperate. "I'll try anything. Send for her."

Isis knew that eventually the gods would send for her, so she had her little black bag all packed and ready when the divine messenger arrived to ask for her help. She arrived at Ra's bedside dressed in her finest robes, with a wide lapis lazuli collar and heavy green eyeshadow. She took his pulse, looked at his tongue, listened to his heart, and shook her head.

"You're in a bad way, Pops," she declared. "But you've sent for the right gal. I can help you, but you'll have to cooperate."

Ra groaned. "Anything. Just make the pain go away."

"Well then, you'll have to tell me your secret name."

Ra was horrified. In his name lay all his powers. "I—I can't. I, um, don't have a secret name."

"Ha, don't give me that. All you gods have secret names."

Ra tried to stall. "Well, it's, um, Rumplestiltskin."

"Puleeeze. I wasn't born yesterday. I can see that you don't want to be cured." Isis packed up her little black bag and headed for the door.

Ra called out feebly, "Wait!" Isis turned and leaned against the doorframe, yawning elaborately. Ra gnashed his teeth and groaned some more. But he was growing weaker. Finally he took a deep breath and whispered his secret name. In doing so he transferred all his power to Isis. Before the old god's rheumy eyes, she grew taller, and wings sprouted from her shoulder blades. She also suddenly got really great hair and her bust size increased by two inches. She had become a goddess, not just your average minor goddess, but the most powerful goddess of the ancient world!

As she flew triumphantly out of the room, Isis snapped her fingers in Ra's direction and cured him instantly. She was nothing if not magnanimous.

Isis AND Osiris

A less obscure legend about Isis portrays her as much nicer than she was when she poisoned Ra to get his power. Of course, at the time of that legend, Isis was already a goddess, so maybe she could afford to be nicer. Her husband Osiris, so the story goes, was killed by the god Set, who was jealous of the handsome god's popularity. Set chopped Osiris up into a hundred pieces, scattering them all over the known world. Isis wandered through the ancient lands, finding the pieces and putting them all back together again, like a grisly jigsaw puzzle. Unfortunately, Osiris' penis had fallen into the ocean and had been swallowed up by a fish, so Isis had to make a gold one for him. Then Isis invented mummification, so that she could wrap her husband up and bring him back to life. And she did—but without the most important part of him, it was only a kind of half-life, so Osiris had to go down to the Underworld and rule there as king of the dead.

Yet another story in which the goddess' main squeeze descends into the Underworld!

Uzume and Amaterasu

You think your brother is obnoxious? Try having the Japanese Storm God for a brother, like Amaterasu, the Sun Goddess, did. No wonder she had a hissy fit! There were no two ways about it, Susanowo was gross and disgusting. It was bad enough on the Earth, where his burps and belches caused foul winds to devastate the rice crops and blow the blossoms from the cherry trees, but he outdid himself when one day he invaded his gorgeous sister's heavenly palace.

Now, we won't mention how he tracked mud and raw sewage all over her nice clean carpet, but it was a dark day in the history of sibling rivalry when he actually pooped on her throne! Afterwards, Susanowo climbed to the top of his sister's golden weaving pavilion and hurled the decaying body of a dead horse through the roof, where it landed with a splatter right on the gleaming tapestry Amaterasu and her delicate white-faced maidens were weaving. Naturally, her maidens were every bit as sensitive as their high-strung mistress, and the most sensitive of them all immediately lay down and died of disgust.

This was the last straw for Amaterasu. "That's it, I've had it." she declared. "I don't even think he's really my brother. He was probably adopted."

While her surviving maidens cowered and wept into delicate lace hankies, she marched out of the ruined weaving hall, head high. Her long black hair and the hem of her scarlet kimono trailed behind her as she entered the Cave of Heaven, the Ama No Iwayato. Pulling the heavy door shut behind her, she slumped into a corner.

"I'm not going to take it anymore," she added to no one in particular. She then took from her sleeve a copy of Lady Murasaki's novel, *The Tale of Genji,* and proceeded to read.

Now, this was all well and good for Amaterasu, but when the sun goddess shut the door of the Cave of Heaven, the sun went out. Instantly, the Earth below was plunged into pitch darkness. Deprived of life-giving sunlight, fruit died on the trees, crops withered, and people starved. Cries from the wretched mortals below soon reached the gods and goddesses in heaven, all 8 million of them. The worried dieties banged on the door of the cave.

"Um, Amaterasu, we hate to disturb you, but people are, you know, dying? Do you think maybe you could, like, come out now?"

Amaterasu called back, "Go away and leave me alone. And furthermore, I don't want to talk about it."

The deities huddled together in the darkness outside the cave, worried and panicky.

"This looks bad," said one. "If Amaterasu doesn't come out, the Earth will die. And without people, there'll be no one to worship us."

Uzume, the goddess of merriment, spoke up. She was a short, round little creature who wore an extra-large kimono.

"Listen. Moaning won't help. We need a plan, and I have one."

A few hours later, the 8 million deities met again in front of the Cave of Heaven. This time they brought with them an odd assortment of noisemakers: drums, cymbals, horns, rattles, and an enormous gong. Next to the cave entrance, they hung a polished

Amaterasu, the Japanese sun goddess

brass mirror from a tree. Uzume had also brought along a tin washtub; she upended it and then climbed on top of it.

Standing still for a moment, Uzume asked herself, "Are you sure you want to go ahead with this? You're hardly a super-model, you know."

But after thinking it over, she told herself, "Hey, it's my body and I'm proud of it." And with that she signaled the band to start.

Then, as some of the deities slowly banged on their drums, Uzume started to dance. She knew all the moves; she had practiced them alone in her celestial bedroom.

At first all the gods and goddesses were hushed, watching as Uzume's nimble feet kept up with the drumbeats. As drums beat faster, Uzume shrugged off one sleeve of her extra-large sized kimono. When the gods with rattles joined in, Uzume then slipped off her other sleeve. All of the deities clapped in time to the beat.

Uzume strutted around and tossed her fabulous hair. She then untied her sash, flung it into the crowd, and coyly opened her kimono, flashing first one side and then the other. The gods and goddesses screamed in anticipation. Finally, she let the kimono slide off, throwing it into the crowd, but she was wearing another robe beneath it.

Now the horns added their wailing notes to the music.

Uzume shook her big hips and let her backbone slip. The gods and goddesses clapped and stamped their feet. She winked and wiggled her tongue at them, then lifted the hem of her robe to flash some thigh.

The crowd went wild. Eight million goddesses and gods shouted, "You go, girl!" and "Take it off!" And Uzume did. Shrugging out of the sleeves, she held the robe over her chest. Cymbals clashed and she gave the gods a peek at one brown nipple. She lifted up the back of her robe, mooning the audience. They loved it! No one had ever seen a striptease before. Then, as the strongest god pounded on the giant brass gong, Uzume took it all off, and danced for the gods stark naked, her various body parts bouncing.

The whistles and catcalls of the 8 million gods reached Amaterasu where she sat reading *The Tale of Genji* in the Cave of Heaven. The hubbub was impossible to ignore. She put down the book, strode to the door and shouted, "Can you please keep it down out there? I'm trying to read!"

Of course they all ignored her. Actually, they couldn't even hear her over their own clamor. This was too much for Amaterasu, who was used to having her major sulks catered to. Anyway, she wondered, what were they all carrying on about? Slowly she opened the cave door so she could see what was going on.

"In the name of Me!" she exclaimed. "That's Uzume, dancing on an upturned tub. And she's totally naked! How disgusting. If I had Uzume's figure, I'd stay at home and never go out at all! "

Amaterasu opened the cave door just a little wider and added, "Maybe I'll just watch this for a *second*." But there were 8 million gods and goddesses in the way, so she opened the door wide for a better view, and found herself staring into the polished brass mirror that hung from the tree in front of her cave.

If you can believe this, Amaterasu had never seen herself in a mirror before. Maybe it had been enough to hear 8 million gods and goddesses tell her that she looked great in whatever she wore. She was fascinated by what she saw. "Who," she breathed, "is this magnificent person? Why aren't the gods applauding her instead of that little piece of trash, Uzume?"

Entranced by the gorgeous creature in the mirror, she stepped out of the cave for a closer look. This was what the gods and goddesses had been waiting for. The two strongest rolled a big boulder into the entrance, so that Amaterasu couldn't get back in. As soon as she was out of the cave, Earth warmed up. Spring came again, buds burst into flower, green shoots poked their way up from the ground, people crept out of hiding, and all the gods and goddesses breathed a collective sigh of relief.

As for Susanowo, after his fingernails and toenails were pulled out, he was banished to Earth, to the delight of the gods, if not the mortals. With her gross brother out of the way, Amaterasu was content to remain out of the cave. Her emblem, the rising sun, shines from the Japanese flag and her mirror can be seen in Shinto shrines across Japan.

THE *Goddess* OF *Exotic Dancers*

Traditionally, Japan's emperors have always claimed to be descended from Amaterasu. Just as traditionally, the exotic dancers of the world ought to recognize their own ancestress: Uzume, fat and proud, the world's first stripper.

Three

Bad Girls of the Bible

Lilith

Don't believe everything you read in the Bible. For instance, who says Eve was the first woman? The fact is, before God pulled Eve from Adam's side in the form of a rib, he made Lilith as Adam's mate, making them both at the same time, out of the same earth. He then put them in the Garden of Eden and said, "Go on, now, have a good time. Be fruitful, multiply, and name the animals."

Adam looked at Lilith and she was a stunner. Lilith looked at Adam and thought, You're not half-bad yourself, big boy. Unfortunately, due to their very different personalities, this was not a marriage made in heaven. You see, Lilith had this habit of speaking up for herself.

Trouble started almost immediately during the naming of the animals. Adam pointed to one of the animals, and said, "I'll name you *Hippopotamus*."

"Don't be silly," said Lilith. "Hippos don't have curly hair and funny haircuts with little pink bows, nor do they balance on their hind paws. That's a poodle, if I ever saw one."

"But I already named that one Poodle!" Adam pointed to another animal.

Lilith let out a snort of derision. "You mean the camel? You called that a poodle? Adam, do me a favor, leave the naming to me."

Adam pouted. "I don't know, *poodle* just sounded to me like something with humps on its back." He wasn't happy, but he let her have her way.

It was in bed that things got really bad. Adam started to climb on top of Lilith, and pushing him off, she shouted, "What, are you out of your mind? Let me up this minute!"

Adam stammered, "B-but we're doing the Thing—you know, the Sex Thing, and the man is supposed to be on top."

"Oh yeah? Who says? Adam, you just invented sexism!" Lilith laughed. "Come on, let me get on top, and we'll Do It."

Adam got huffy. "I don't see what's so funny. Anyway, I'm not in the mood anymore."

"Ooh, did I bruise your little male ego?"

Things went on like this for days, and they still hadn't Done It, because they couldn't agree on a position. When Adam insisted that he was superior, and therefore had to be on top, Lilith reminded him, "We were made at exactly the same time, and from the same earth. We're *equals*, babe. Can you get that through your head?"

Adam, who was passive-aggressive anyway, just sulked, but Lilith, who had a short fuse, eventually blew up. "I don't need this! Adam, I left you some passionfruit salad in the cooler. Have a good life. I'm out of here!"

Then she called out the holy and ineffable name of God, and flew away. Adam was crushed. First of all, he had never even known that there was a holy and ineffable name of God! He complained to his maker. "That woman you made was nothing but trouble, and now she's dumped me. Plus, how come you never taught *me* your holy and ineffable name?"

God hemmed and hawed. The truth of the matter was that Lilith could blink her big almond eyes and wheedle secrets out of everyone, even God. But He wanted to keep Adam happy, so He sent three angels, Senoy, Sansenoy, and Semangelof, to fetch Lilith back. They found her living in a cave by the Red Sea. She was having a great time, partying with various demons, all of whom were better in bed than Adam.

When the angels entered the cave, Lilith was making out hot and heavy with two demons at the same time. Senoy cleared his throat loudly. Lilith looked up. "We don't want any," she said, and turned back to the demons, who were really cute, if you overlooked their cloven hooves.

Senoy cleared his throat again and Lilith, getting annoyed, shouted, "What?"

Sansenoy said, "We've come to take you back to Adam."

Semangelof muttered under his breath, "If he could see you acting like a tramp, he wouldn't want you back."

Senoy elbowed Semangelof in the side and said, "Really, Adam misses you."

Lilith laughed derisively. "Yeah, right. You want me to go back and become some meek little housewife? Give me a break! We're having a good time here!" And she pinched one of the demons on his cheek. "Aren't we, snookums?"

The angels were shocked. They hadn't expected her to refuse. "But you have to go back to Adam!" exclaimed Sansenoy. "We'll make you go back!"

"You and what army?" demanded Lilith. "What can you do to me if I won't go?"

"We'll—we'll kill you!"

Lilith tossed her hair. "Oh, grow up. You can't kill me. I happen to be immortal."

And it was true! Because Lilith had left Adam before that unfortunate incident with the apple, she continued to be immortal, even after Adam and Eve were evicted from Eden and given a mortal life span. Defeated, the angels left the cave with drooping wings.

As for Lilith, she became queen of the demons and stuck around through the centuries, creating women's music festivals and also taking the form of a succubus, who visited men in their sleep and stole their precious bodily fluids. When a guy had a wet dream or a nocturnal emission, he claimed it was because Lilith had climbed on top of him while he slept. Isn't that just like a man? Ever since Adam, they've been blaming the woman.

Lilith and Adam in the Garden of Eden

Banned FROM THE *Bible*

Like Rome, the Old Testament wasn't built in a day. Actually, it was composed in bits and pieces over a span of more than 500 years, by a bunch of guys with long beards. Eventually this collection of the different myths and legends got messy, so they had to decide what to keep in and what to leave out. The result was the Canon, or officially accepted twenty-four books (more like chapters, really) that make up the Old Testament. Guess who got left out? Although there are still hints in the Old Testament of a first wife who was made equally and at the same time as Adam ("Male and female created He them."), the next page finds God putting Adam to sleep, removing one of his ribs and making it into a woman. And voilà, after that it's all Eve, no Lilith!

So if she's not in the Bible, how do we know about her? Lilith has existed in myth and folklore for centuries, but the oldest version of her story is in a manuscript called the *Alphabet of Ben Sira*, which dates from somewhere between the seventh and tenth centuries. Why did those bearded guys leave Lilith out of the Old Testament? Are you kidding? When women read her story, they might have gotten ideas, not the least of which was, "You mean there are *other* positions?"

Judith

Back in the Old Testament days, a young widow named Judith lived in the city of Bethulia, which was one of those ancient cities like Nineveh and Tyre, that archaeologists are always trying to dig up in the middle of the Middle Eastern desert. She was a J.A.P., or Jewish Ancient Princess. Her husband had left her loaded. She had gold and silver, precious gems, designer dresses that she didn't have to buy on sale, tons of servants at her beck and call, and to top it all off, she looked like a supermodel.

All of Judith's wealth, however, was of no help to her or anyone else, when the Assyrian General Holofernes laid siege to the city with his army of 120,000 foot soldiers and 12,000 cavalry, cutting off the city's water and food supply. By the thirty-fourth day of the siege the water had given out, the food was running low, and people were fainting in the streets. Things looked bad, and Bethulia was on the verge of surrender. But not Judith.

Judith had that famous Jewish trait known as chutzpah. Bathing herself in jasmine-scented oils, and dressing up in her golden sandals and designer silks, she had her maid do her hair up in the latest style, topping it with a tiara. She then proceeded to the mayor's house.

Now, the mayor and the city council were in a meeting, trying to figure out how much longer they could hold out, when Judith marched in. Batting her green-painted eyelids at the politicians, who of course were all men with long beards, she climbed to the dais and addressed them. In those days, men weren't all that ready to listen to a mere woman, but Judith was so easy on the eyes that they made an exception.

"You call yourselves *menches*?" she scolded them, "Are you gonna let us wait around until we all die of hunger and thirst? Well, not me. I have a plan."

A plan? The men all stroked their beards and muttered to each other. Finally the mayor asked Judith, "Um, What kind of plan?"

"Don't ask," she answered. "Only let me and my maid out of the city, so we can find our way to Holofernes' camp, and you'll see."

The mayor and his council shrugged. What did they have to

lose? The guards opened the city gates and let Judith and her maid out. Judith's maid, Abra, carried two big baskets loaded with food, lots of strong wine, and a few changes of clothes—you couldn't expect Judith to appear in the same outfit twice!—and they made their way to the enemy camp.

All 120,000 foot soldiers and 12,000 cavalry stared at the pretty Jewish girl and her maid. At Judith's request, the astonished Assyrian sentries led her straight to the general's purple tent, where he lounged on cushions beneath embroidered hangings, munching on grapes. His sword, razor-sharp and brightly polished, hung above his bed. He almost choked on a grape seed when Judith sashayed in, followed by Abra.

"Hello, handsome, " she breathed huskily. "I heard you were the hunkiest soldier in all of Assyria, and I see that it's true. I'm just Judith, a poor li'l ole widow, who has come to surrender to you, and to help you invade Bethulia."

Now, Holofernes was anything but handsome, as he bore the scars of a fighting man. His nose was flattened and a white scar ran diagonally across his face. Plus he had the body of an over-the-hill weightlifter and had acquired an enormous beer belly. But he was vain. He had slicked his hair back with goat grease and perfumed his beard. His favorite slave girl gave him manicures. So he chose to believe what Judith said.

Gesturing toward the dinner table, upon which was set an

entire roasted pig with an apple in its mouth, he said, "Come, join me for dinner, and tell me your plan."

Judith looked at the pig and curled her lip in disdain. "Are you kidding? That's not kosher. Anyway, I'm on a diet, and I've brought my own food. But if you'll show me and my maid to my tent, we can talk some more tomorrow."

On her way out of Holofernes' tent, Judith stopped, turned, and added, "Oh, by the way, I hope you don't mind, but every day I'll have to leave your camp and bathe in that pool in the valley. It has crystal clear water, very good for the skin. A girl like me, alone in the world, has to look nice, you know."

The general was so taken by surprise that all he could do was give Judith her way. But as he sent her off to her own tent he thought, "If I have my way, you won't sleep alone every night, pretty Jewish girl."

For three days, Judith slept alone in her tent. Each day she left the Assyrian camp to wash in the pool in the valley, but that's not all she did. Unknown to Holofernes, after her bath she would proceed to the gates of Bethulia and leave a message with the guards.

"Just a few days more," she told them. "Trust me."

Then she'd return to the camp and have a nice chat with Holofernes. "Just a few days more," she'd tell him. "The Bethulians will be reduced to eating the dogs and cats in the

street. Your army can march in and take them without losing a
man. Trust me."

Then Judith would get up to return to her tent. Holofernes
would try to pull her down onto the pile of cushions, but she'd
shrug him off, murmuring, "What's your hurry, big boy? There'll
be plenty of time for *that* later."

On the fourth day, Holofernes grew impatient. "This is
ridiculous," he muttered angrily to himself. "That pretty Jewish
girl's been sleeping alone for four days, and I still haven't known
her in the biblical sense. By now the whole camp's probably
laughing at me."

And he sent a messenger to Judith. "You're invited to dinner
with the general, and he won't take no for an answer."

"I wouldn't dream of refusing the general," breathed Judith.
"Why, I've been waiting for this day all my life. But let my maid
cook us up something kosher—a nice chicken—and I insist on
bringing the wine."

Judith had saved her best dress for last, and she slipped into
it. It was shinier, tighter, and filmier than any of her others. Gold
on her wrists, around her neck, and in her earlobes, some
Egyptian-style eye makeup, and she was ready. She undulated
into Holofernes' tent along with Abra, who brought the chicken
and lots of strong Jewish wine in her basket.

Abra set the table and waited outside, leaving Judith and

Holofernes alone in the tent. Judith settled into the cushions and offered him a chicken leg. She smiled up at him. "A shekel for your thoughts," she murmured.

Holofernes had never really had to talk to his women before. He stuttered and stammered a bit, until Judith held out a goblet filled to the brim with strong purple drink. "Have some wine," she offered.

Relieved, the Assyrian general drained the goblet. "Hey, that's not bad," he said. "A bit sweet, but not bad."

"Have some more," said Judith.

After draining quite a few more goblets, Holofernes had no trouble talking. He told Judith how his father had never really liked him, how his concubines didn't understand him, how he was really a sensitive person who loved kittens and puppies, and that it was quite painful for him when he was forced to torture prisoners of war.

"Tsk, tsk," said Judith. "More wine?"

After draining even more goblets, Holofernes was telling Judith she was the best friend he had ever had in his whole life,

Judith and Holofernes— or what's left of him!

when he fell over into the pile of cushions and started snoring loudly. This was what she had been waiting for. Reaching over the comatose general, she removed his sword from the wall above his bed. She shut her eyes, took a deep breath, and, holding the sword in both hands, brought it down with all her strength on Holofernes' neck. When she opened her eyes, the general was in two parts: his head and the rest of him.

Judith called her maid in, and between the two of them they managed to get the disgusting head into the big basket. They covered it with cloth, and tried to look casual as they walked out of the camp.

"Gotta wash up in that pool," Judith told the sentries. "A midnight bath, you know. Really good for the complexion."

The sentries, used to her comings and goings, let her through. Judith and Abra went straight to Bethulia. "It's me, Judith," she called to the city guards. "Guess what I have?"

As you can imagine, all of Bethulia went wild. They hung the head of Holofernes from their gate, thereby scaring off the entire Assyrian army, who fled when they realized their general had been killed by one pretty Jewish girl.

As for Abra, Judith bought her a nice little dress shop and set her up in business. Judith herself remained a heroine all her life, which lasted 105 years. She never married again, not that lots of nice Jewish boys didn't ask, but just in case Bethulia was ever threatened again, she wanted to be free to do what a girl's gotta do.

Raging Women OF THE Renaissance

This painting is by the seventeenth-century artist Artemisia Gentileschi. A woman artist in Renaissance Italy was a *rara avis* indeed, and Artemisia went her few contemporary women artists one better—she stood up for herself. To begin with, Artemisia was lucky to be the daughter of Orazio Gentileschi, a successful Italian painter who taught his daughter everything he knew; women weren't allowed into art school in those days. Artemisia started as her father's apprentice, but before long she was a famous painter in her own right.

Enter a mediocre artist named Agostino Tassi, who had designs on the illustrious Gentileschi name and the fame and fortune that went with it. His unorthodox method of getting Artemisia to marry him was to rape her. He figured she'd have to marry him in order to save her reputation. (It so happened that Agostino already had a wife, whom he had deserted years before, but that didn't seem to bother him.)

What Agostino didn't count on was that Artemisia not only refused to marry him, but brought him to court for rape. This was a shocker because in those days, once it was known that a girl had been raped, her reputation was ruined. Artemisia didn't care; she demanded justice. Agostino's defense was that Artemisia was a whore who'd already had sex with scads of men. At the trial, Artemisia was actually tortured, to make sure she spoke the truth!

Renaissance women didn't have counseling and rape crisis hotlines. To make matters worse, despite the outcome of the trial (Agostino was found guilty), Artemisia was the subject of snickering, innuendo-filled verses. It's almost impossible to imagine the extent of Artemisia's rage, but here's a hint: She painted Judith beheading Holofernes over and over and *over*. There are at least *six* known versions of the painting done by her.

By the way, like Lilith, Judith's story was excluded from the Old Testament.

Artemisia Gentileschi, Judith Slaying Holofernes

Jezebel

In about 800 B.C.E., in the land of Israel, prophets were coming out of the woodwork. These were mostly skinny, bearded guys in sandals and sackcloth, who went around prophesying doom because, they said, everybody but them was wicked. Their definition of *wicked* was anybody who had any fun, especially including women who wore too much makeup, worshiped the goddess, and in general were not Nice Jewish Girls.

Jezebel, wife of Ahab, king of the Israelites, fitted the definition of wicked five ways from Sunday, and those bearded guys were not happy with her at all. Actually, that's an understatement. This new queen represented everything they hated. Jezebel was not a Nice Jewish Girl. She was a high priestess of the goddess Astarte, and her father, King Ethbaal, was a priest of Baal. Plus, she went a little too heavy with the war paint. The ancient Hebrew prophets were bitterly opposed to makeup and any gods or goddesses except Jehovah.

In fact, Jezebel was the matriarch of a line of strong women rulers. Her niece, Dido, became queen of Carthage, and her daughter, Athaliah, was the only other woman besides Jezebel to rule Israel. (Jezebel also inspired a terrific movie starring Bette Davis, but that was later.) None of this endeared her to Elijah, the sternest and most patriarchal of the stern and patriarchal prophets of doom, who didn't like strong women. He made a real pest of himself, leading a small parade of prophets up and down in front of the palace, wearing sandwich boards proclaiming Jezebel the Whore of Babylon (which was incorrect because Jezebel came from the Phoenician city of Tyre), and shouting, "Harlot!" at the top of their lungs. You really can't blame Jezebel for getting so annoyed that she persecuted the whole noisy crew, and managed to have many of them killed before the others fled, hiding out in caves in the desert. Elijah retaliated by inciting an angry mob to tear apart all of Jezebel's 450 high priests, so queen and prophet were evenly matched.

King Ahab was as weak as Jezebel was strong, and a bit of a spoiled brat into the bargain. Growing up as a prince, and with a Jewish mother, he had always gotten his way, and expected things to continue in that vein.

One day he approached a man named Naboth, who owned a vineyard near the palace, and offered to buy it from him. "I'll pay anything, plus I'll relocate you to some other neighborhood," he told Naboth. "That land of yours is right below my window and I'd like to turn it into a garden. What do you say?"

Naboth answered, "Sorry, your highness, but that vineyard was owned by my father, and before that by his father, and it has sentimental value. I can't part with it."

Ahab went back to the palace and sulked. Around

Jezebel

dinnertime, Jezebel noticed that he was missing and she went looking for him. She found him lying on his bed, face turned to the wall.

"Honeybun," she said, "Dinner's ready, and I had the cook prepare your favorite pot roast. Aren't you coming?"

"Not hungry," muttered Ahab.

Jezebel sighed. Men were such children! "Okay, what's wrong this time?" she asked.

"Naboth won't sell me his vineyard. And I want that vineyard!"

Jezebel couldn't believe the fuss he was making over such a silly thing. "Is that all? You're a king, you can just take the vineyard!"

Ahab sniffed, "Can't."

Jezebel shrugged her white shoulders. Ahab could be impossible to deal with sometimes. She proceeded to her writing desk, took up parchment and quill, and penned a declaration: "Be it hereby known that one Naboth, owner of the vineyard below King Ahab's window, has blasphemed King Ahab and Jehovah, and ought to be stoned to death." Then she forged Ahab's name to the document, sealed it with his seal, and sent it out to the multitudes, who dutifully stoned the hapless Naboth to death.

Jezebel sashayed back to the bedroom where Ahab still lay in a snit, and chirped, "Okay, dear, Naboth is dead, and the vineyard is yours. Now come to dinner."

Ahab exclaimed, "Goody!" and ran out to claim his new property, but a furious Elijah blocked his path.

"Evil!" ranted the prophet, "Worshiper of false gods and husband of a harlot! The dogs will lick thy blood, and as for thy tramp of a wife, the dogs will eat her!"

Ahab fled back to the palace and cowered in his room, but Jezebel sent for Elijah and banished him. "And if you set foot in Israel again, your life won't be worth a plugged shckel," she screamed.

In the tradition of men throughout history, Ahab declared war on a small country—in this case, Syria—in order to salvage his self-esteem. Not much of a soldier, he was wounded in battle, bled all over his chariot, and died. When the chariot was washed out, dogs came and licked up the blood and water that dripped onto the ground, thus fulfilling Elijah's prophesy.

Queen Jezebel now ruled Israel along with her grandson, Ahaziah, but she got no rest. The fighting that Ahab had started escalated, so that soon Israel was at war with the country of Moab as well as Syria. Meanwhile, Elijah had gone up to heaven in a chariot of fire, but another prophet, Elisha, younger but just as rabid, took his place, picketing the palace and calling Jezebel a harlot. Elisha approached Jehu, a captain of Jezebel's army, announcing, "Guess what? Jehovah just told me that you can be the next king of Israel. All you have to do is slay that slut, Jezebel, and her grandson."

Jehu went, "Cool," and gathered an army to invade the palace. Today we call this a military coup, but Jehu simply insisted that God was on his side.

Jezebel and Ahaziah looked out their palace window and saw Jehu in his chariot, riding hellbent for leather and leading the entire army against them. Ahaziah saddled up his horse and tried to make a break for it, but one of Jehu's arrows got him right through the heart. As for Jezebel, her lip curled up with scorn for her grandson. "The men in this family are all weaklings," she declared, and went to meet her unavoidable death in a manner befitting a proud queen. She slathered on the makeup with a palette knife, knowing this would infuriate Elisha, who was probably watching the whole scene from behind some bushes. Then she had a maid do up her

hair and top it with her best tiara. She put on a fabulous designer gown and all of her jewelry, and sat at window, waiting for Jehu.

Jehu drew up his chariot below the window and shouted up at the palace, "Who's on my side?" Two eunuchs, probably harboring deep resentment against Jezebel because she had them castrated, shouted, "We are!" They came up behind the queen and pushed her out the window. She fell in front of Jehu, who crushed her beneath his chariot wheels.

Then he marched into the palace and demanded that a feast be set before him. After he'd eaten and drunk his fill, he remembered Jezebel.

"Go get her body" he commanded, "She was no good, but I suppose we have to bury her as befits a queen."

But all that his servants could find was the palms of her hands. As Elijah had prophesied, the dogs had eaten all the rest.

History IS WRITTEN BY THE Winners

If you read the story of Jezebel in the Bible, it seems that her worst sin (except for a heavy hand with the Max Factor) was that nasty incident of the vineyard. Jezebel, the Bible tells us, wrote the proclamation that got poor Naboth killed, then forged Ahab's signature to it. Yeah, right. What proof do we have that Ahab didn't write the proclamation and sign it himself? Jezebel can't tell us her side of the story, because she's been thrown out of her window, crushed beneath chariot wheels, and eaten by dogs. We have to take the word of the survivors, a bunch of goddess-haters who had it in for Jezebel because she was a high priestess of Astarte. And by the way, those skinny bearded guys, who were not crazy about strong women, didn't much like Jezebel's daughter, Queen Athaliah, or her niece Queen Dido, either, and voted them off the island.

Unfortunately, history has always been written by the winners.

four

Sorceresses:
Don't Drink That!

Cerridwen

The Welsh sorceress Cerridwen was a single mother who lived with her son and daughter on a small island in the middle of Lake Tegid. Nobody ever said a sorceress couldn't be a good mother, and Cerridwen was one of the best, a regular mama bear. Her daughter, Creidwy, was the prettiest girl in the world, with golden curls, glittering blue eyes shaded by long lashes, and cheeks and smiling lips red as ripe apples. Her son, Afagdu, was another story entirely. The poor child, chinless and beady-eyed, with sparse, lank, colorless hair and the tubby body of a piglet, was unbelievably homely, so Cerridwen was very protective of him.

"In fact," admitted Cerridwen sadly, "even through the loving eyes of his mother, I fear that he is the ugliest boy in the world." Of course, she didn't say this where Afagdu would hear her; the poor kid had enough problems.

Cerridwen watched through her tower window as the wretched child, still unaware of his misfortune, played outside with his beautiful sister. "You'll have a terrible time of it when you grow up," she mused. "After all, you can't stay on this island forever. Nobody will give you a decent job. Babies will scream when they see you. And you'll never get girls. What to do?"

But Cerridwen was a sorceress, so she didn't ponder the question for long. Quickly she got to work, combing the island for just the right herbs with which to concoct a brew for her son. She couldn't make him handsome, but she could even the odds by making him the smartest boy in the world. While she was at it, she gathered some snakes and amphibians to give the brew extra punch. She built a fire under a big iron cauldron. Then, following a recipe in her great-great-grandmother's spell-book, she tossed in the ingredients: adder's tongue and frog warts, Echinacea for good health, gingko biloba and ginseng for the brain, St. John's wort to give the boy higher self-esteem, a pinch of amanita muscara and rye mold for the imagination, garlic for flavoring, a generous helping of chicken necks and chicken feet because they're good for you, and of course the most potent ingredient, mandrake root. (Warning: Do not try this at home!)

Then she frowned. "Hmmm ... the recipe calls for this to be stirred constantly as it boils for a year and a day. Who has the time? I'll have to hire someone."

Cerridwen rowed across the lake to the shore, where she saw a young boy tending his sheep. "Yoo hoo, boy!" she called out. "Would you like to earn some money?" And she held up four gold coins.

The boy, whose name was Gwion Bach, was thrilled. Four gold coins was more than he expected to see in his whole life-time, so he left the sheep and went back with Cerridwen to her island. She put him to work stirring the bubbling brew with a long wooden spoon, and went about her business, taking care of her children, growing esoteric herbs and spices in her garden, and stewing batches of magic potion in smaller pots and pans. Gwion was all too happy to spend the next year doing nothing but stirring a boiling pot, taking five minutes off now and then for a sandwich. When his arm grew tired, he just thought about the four pieces of gold and switched arms. And every now and then Cerridwen would come over, taste for flavor and sprinkle in a little salt or pepper.

But Cerridwen's sundial was a bit slow, so she didn't realize that the year and the day were up, when three drops of magic

Cerridwen, the Welsh sorceress

brew bubbled up out of the cauldron and splashed onto Gwion's thumb. The boy put his scalded thumb into his mouth, and immediately became the smartest boy in the world! He knew everything—including the fact that once Cerridwen realized that he had taken the magic reserved for her own son, she would be so furious that she'd want to kill him. Gwion started to run, and not a moment too soon, because suddenly all hell broke loose. Once the three magic drops had escaped, all that was left in the cauldron was a deadly poison that split the cauldron into a hundred pieces. Cerridwen, memorizing magic spells in her tower, heard the explosion and realized what had happened. As Gwion had guessed, she raged, "That little thief! I work my fingers to the bone making a magic potion for my son, and he steals it! Killing's too good for him, but it'll have to do!" And she took off in hot pursuit of the fleeing boy.

Gwion's brain had expanded to the point where he was one up on Einstein, so he now knew as much magic as Cerridwen. When he saw her chasing him, he turned himself into the fastest creature he could think of—a rabbit—and hopped away. But for all his new-gotten wisdom, Cerridwen was still older and craftier. She turned herself into a bloodhound and gave chase. She had almost caught up with Gwion when he reached the lake's edge, hopped into the water, and swam away as a salmon. Cerridwen jumped into the water too, took the form of an otter, and swam after him. "I'll get you yet, my little pretty," she called in otter language.

Just when the otter's mouth was wide open to gulp down the fish, Gwion rose from the water in the shape of a small bird and flew away into the sky. Of course, Cerridwen wasn't that easily beaten. She became a hawk and flew after him. The little bird flew as fast as its little wings would carry it, but still the hawk was gaining. He was almost caught within the hawk's talons when they flew over a barn and Gwion turned into a grain of wheat, dropping down through a hole in the thatched roof. He landed upon the floor among the other scattered seeds.

As he lay there, trying hard to be just another grain of wheat, a black hen wandered into the barn, pecking at the grains to the right and left of her. It was Cerridwen in the form of a chicken. If a grain of wheat can shiver, Gwion shivered. He attempted to be as still and wheatlike as possible, but a good sorceress, even when she's a chicken, can feel the vibes of another human being, and Cerridwen walked right up to him on her chicken feet and towered over him.

"Steal magic from my son, will you?" she clucked, and she gobbled him up.

Gwion remained inside of Cerridwen for nine months, during which time she entered her daughter in the Little Miss Ancient Wales beauty contest, and enrolled her son in a very good private school where, with the aid of her various herbs and spells, he became a prize pupil. Then after nine months she gave birth to Gwion in the form of a baby boy. Cerridwen was such a good mother that she couldn't bear to kill the beautiful infant. "But," she said, "damned if I'm gonna raise up this little thief as my own son." So she wrapped him up and put him in a little boat, which she set afloat.

The little boat made it to shore, and the baby was found and adopted by a prince. Under his new name, Taliesin, the boy once called Gwion became the most famous poet and prophet in ancient Wales. There's a moral here: If a sorceress gets mad at you, try to appeal to her maternal instinct.

Fertility Drugs OF THE Ancient World

Cerridwen giving birth to little Gwion after swallowing him as a grain of wheat isn't as unusual as it sounds. Women in mythology had a way of getting pregnant after swallowing all sorts of strange things. Etain, a beautiful Irish maiden, beloved of Midir, lord of the fairies, was turned into a purple fly by Midir's jealous wife. The fly fell into a golden cup full of wine and was swallowed by an Irish princess, who then gave birth to her, and named the baby girl Etain. Quite a coincidence! The story gets really complicated after she grows up, when Midir shows up and wants his true love back. Etain's new husband tells Midir he can have Etain if he can pick her out of a crowd of women who all look alike. Midir thinks he has picked out Etain, only to be informed that the woman he chose is actually Etain's daughter, named—that's right—Etain!

Dahut

During the period when Christianity was just beginning to take hold in Europe, the ancient city of Ys stood next to the sea in that part of Brittany known as Finisterre, in the area which is now known as France. Finisterre means "the End of the World," so that should tell you a little something about Ys. In fact, the only thing that kept the city from being under water was a great sea wall that the king, Gradlon, had constructed between his city and the greedy waves.

Gradlon was one of those geezers with a dusty gray beard who kept his nose into his dusty library of books day and night. Once upon a time he must have been young and cute, because the mother of his dark-haired darling daughter, the princess Dahut, was a fairy, and generally fairies don't get the hots for dusty geezers.

Dahut's mother, the sea fairy

One day at the edge of town, the missionary Saint Gwenole showed up and built himself a little monastery. He then proceeded to convert everyone in Ys to Christianity, except for Gradlon's half-fairy daughter, Dahut. Saint Gwenole didn't trust Dahut farther than he could throw her, and he was right. The girl was simply no good.

One day Dahut ambled into the study where her father sat day and night, buried in his books, and said, "*Bonjour*, Papa. May I have the tower room to dabble in the Black Arts?"

Without looking up, Gradlon answered, "Anything you say, dear, but don't bother me now, I'm reading."

Like you're not always reading, thought Dahut, but she

curtsied, lifting the velvet skirts of her pre-Raphaelite gown and said, "*Merci*, Papa." Then she climbed the winding staircase to the tower, redecorated it all in purple and black, and proceeded to sacrifice a thing or two to the Dark Forces.

Pretty soon Dahut developed a habit of picking up dark, curly-haired village boys and bringing them up to her tower room to spend the night. This was okay, except that they were never seen again. Eventually the people of Ys noticed that there were no more hunks left in the village, and they started muttering among themselves. They sent an emissary to Saint Gwenole, who was not the least bit surprised. "I knew that girl was no good," he said, and he went to where Gradlon sat in his library, immersed in arcane manuscripts. "Your Highness," said the monk, "I don't mean to bother you, but it seems as though your daughter, the Princess Dahut, is sacrificing the young men of the village."

The king didn't even look up. "Could we take this up another time?" he asked. "I'm just getting to the good part."

Saint Gwenole sighed, exclaimed, "Ooh la la!," shrugged his Gallic shoulders, and retired to his monastery to pray.

Meanwhile Dahut, having used up all the village boy-toys, tried her hand at sacrificing black roosters, but it wasn't as much fun. She tried shopping, but the good boutiques were all in Paris, and she was too young to go there on her own—did I mention that she was only sixteen? So she sat at her tower window, overlooking the village and the hungry sea, drumming her fingers on the stone ledge.

"I'll go mad with boredom," she told herself, not realizing that she was already quite mad. "There's absolutely nothing to do in this one-horse town. Ys might as well be under the ocean for all the fun I have here."

And then Dahut got an idea.

Taking the winding stone steps two at a time, she raced down to her father's study, where she found him—surprise!—surrounded by books. "Bonjour, Papa," she panted. "You know the big brass key that opens the floodgates to the sea wall that keeps the ocean away from our city? Do you think I could have that key?"

The king sighed, adjusted his silver-rimmed glasses, turned a page, but of course he did not look up. "Whatever you'd like, dear, but don't disturb me, I've come to a really hot sex scene."

Dahut curtsied and murmured, "Merci, Papa." Then she plucked the key from the brass hook where it hung on the wall and ran down to the edge of the village. "Now we'll see a little excitement," she said to herself, turning the key in its rusty lock, and pushing open the great stone seagate. Saltwater poured in, and Dahut lifted her scarlet brocade skirts out of the wet. Giggling, she raced the waves back to her castle and up the stairs to her tower. There she leaned out the window, sipping a café au lait and watching as the screaming villagers below, clutching their babies and their belongings, ran for high ground while Ys slowly sank beneath the ocean.

Gradlon was so interested in the sex scene he was reading that he didn't notice anything wrong until first his velvet-slippered feet and then his silk-covered knees grew wet. Then he looked down and realized that his library was slowly filling up with seawater, and that his books were already floating on the foam. "Call a plumber!" he shouted. Then he looked out the window at his half-drowned city and added, "Guess not."

Quickly the king gathered up his favorite books and prepared to flee the city. He was halfway down the stairs when he remembered his daughter, and climbed back upstairs for her. He found the princess still sitting by the window in her black and purple tower room, nibbling on an eclair.

He grabbed her by the arm. "Quick! There's no time to lose! We must escape this city now or we'll drown!"

"Oh," said Dahut. "It didn't occur to me that *we* might be in danger." And stopping only long enough to throw a few favorite things into a hatbox, she fled down the stairs with her father. The water was rising quickly in the stables where Gradlon mounted his fastest steed, with his books in a sack upon his back and his daughter hanging on behind him for dear life. They rode like the wind, trying to outrace the great white-tipped waves that rose from the village below and nipped at the horse's hooves.

But fast as the horse ran, the pursuing waves were just as fast. Suddenly Saint Gwenole floated by them, walking, as saints will, on the water. He called out to the king,"The only way you can survive is by throwing into the water that which you love the most!"

Gradlon groaned, "I hate to do this," but he tossed his precious sack full of books into the water. Nothing happened. Still the waves pursued them.

"Idiot!" yelled Saint Gwenole. "That which you love the most? Hello?"

The king hit himself upside the head and said, "Oh, duh." Then he pushed his daughter off the horse and into the water.

"Merde!" exclaimed Dahut, as the waters closed over her head. But at least she wasn't bored anymore.

The fisherfolk of Brittany say the drowned city of Ys is still there under the water, and that sometimes you can hear the bell of Saint Gwenole's submerged monastery. Knowing that Dahut was half-fairy, and that it's not so easy to kill a fairy, it wouldn't be surprising if the

beautiful but crazed princess was down there too, still plotting her mad escapades.

Bad Babes OF THE Ancient World

Dahut was not the only sorceress to meet a sorry end. As you'll remember from her story, Jezebel, the biblical queen and sorceress, favored heavy makeup and worshiped the ancient goddess. For this she was tossed out of the window by those puritanical bearded Hebrew sages, and was gobbled up by dogs in the street below. If false eyelashes and excessive use of blusher and lip gloss were punishable by defenestration today, we'd have long ago lost Dolly Parton, Cher, and Ru Paul.

Osmotar

The *Kalevala* is a collection of Finnish songs and myths dating back to the days of the Vikings, but the stories are about people who lived in Finland even earlier. They were a hardy folk who spent the short summers hunting, fishing, fighting, and making love, and passed the long dark winters singing songs and getting drunk. But to get drunk you needed beer, and if you can believe the stories, there was a time when beer didn't exist, so someone had to invent it.

In those days everyone knew magic and was either some kind of witch or wizard. Chief among the witches was Louhi, the mistress of North Farm, which stood in the dark, icy regions of Finland's Far North, and that's very far north. The inhabitants of North Farm were rich and successful because Louhi was such an excellent witch, and their wooden farmhouse was so vast that if a cock crowed from the ceiling, you couldn't hear it on the ground, and if a dog barked at the back of the house, you couldn't hear it from the front.

Louhi was bustling about, getting North Farm ready for the biggest event ever: the wedding of her daughter, Osmotar. As she scolded the servants who polished the silver plate, she muttered to herself, "Okay, we slaughtered the biggest steer in the world, but we hardly got anything at all from it; only a hundred tubs of meat, a hundred miles of sausage, and six kegs of suet, but that will have to do. What else needs to be done?"

And she answered herself, "Beer! We need beer so that everyone can get drunk and sing and dance on the table and make fools of themselves. But beer hasn't been invented yet. What will I do?"

Louhi shrugged and announced aloud, "Then I will have to invent it!" The servants, used to Louhi talking out loud to herself, ignored her and went about their polishing.

So Louhi went out to the fields and gathered armfuls of barleycorns and hops, drew buckets of water from the well, and set it all to boil over a good hot fire. She boiled it all summer and all winter before finally pouring the brew into birchwood tubs. Then she tasted it.

Nothing. The brew hadn't fermented; it hadn't become beer yet.

Louhi tore her hair out and screamed with frustration. Her pretty teenage daughter, Osmotar, a rather competent witch herself, tripped lightly over in her little bright little embroidered slippers. "Mom, could you keep it down? I'm trying to concentrate on *The Joy of Sex and Other Premarital Advice.* Anyway, what's the problem?" she asked.

Louhi waved an arm at the tubs. "This is the problem," she wailed. "I'm trying to invent beer, but it isn't working!"

Osmotar said, "Let me give it a try. You go polish some silverware or something." She paced back and forth between the wooden tubs. "It needs something," she mused. "But what?"

There on the floor between the tubs was a wooden splinter. She picked it up and spun around three times widdershins. She murmured, "What would happen if...?"

Osmotar warmed the splinter between her hands and then she inserted it Down There. (Warning; Do not try this at home! It's a very bad place to have splinters!) Immediately, she gave birth to a white squirrel. "Go,

Osmotar

my strange little furry fatherless child," she ordered it. "Climb the tallest tree in the forest on your little furry legs and find me something to put into this brew that will make it ferment."

The squirrel obediently ran to the forest, climbed to the top of the tallest tree, and bit off two pine cones. Clutching them in its little paws, it raced back to Osmotar and put the pine cones in her hands. She looked at them and thought, "Well, maybe. . . ."

She tossed the pine cones into the brew and stirred with a long wooden spoon. Then she waited, and waited, and waited. Finally she tasted.

Nothing. The brew was as flat as before. Osmotar paced some more and pondered, "It still needs something." She looked down, and there on the floor between the tubs was a chip of wood. She picked it up and warmed it between her hands. "You never know," she said to herself. "It just might work." She spun around three times widdershins, and inserted the chip Down There.

This time Osmotar gave birth to a lovely golden-breasted bird. It perched in the palm of her hand and stretched its wings. "Fly away to the top of the highest mountains, my pretty little feathered illegitimate child," she told it, "and bring back something that will make this useless brew foamy."

The bird flew up to the highest mountain peak in the land, and there it found two brown bears fighting with each other,

and foaming at the mouth. "Foam," was the thought in its little birdlike head, so it gathered some of the foaming saliva in its beak and returned to Osmotar.

"This is pretty gross," she said, looking at the rank-smelling bear spit, "but hey, I'll try anything." She poured it into the brew and stirred with a long wooden spoon. She waited, and waited, and waited, and then she tasted it.

Nothing. But Osmotar was too plucky to give up just yet. She paced the floor some more, looking for just the right something, and she spied a little yellow mustard flower growing up from the floorboards. She kneeled down and plucked it. "Promising," she muttered.

Osmotar spun around three times widdershins and inserted the flower You Know Where. This time she gave birth to a tiny yellow and black striped bumblebee. It buzzed around her head as she declared, "My husband-to-be thinks I'm a virgin, and I suppose I am, technically. He doesn't have to know about my unusual—to put it mildly—brood. Go, my tiny offspring, buzz off to the far reaches of this land and return with something that will turn this liquid into beer."

The obedient little bee flew to the end of the land and over nine seas. Halfway to the tenth sea, it came upon an island filled with flowers, and the flowers were filled with honey. It dipped its wings in the honey and flew back over the nine seas, finally falling exhausted onto the tip of Osmotar's little finger.

Osmotar tasted the honey. "Now that's better than bear spit!" she declared, and added it to the brew. She stirred and stirred with a long wooden spoon, and the beer foamed up out of the tubs and overflowed onto the floor. The wedding took place and people drank themselves silly. As for Osmotar's new husband, if he ever wondered about the squirrel, the bird, and the bee that shared their house, he never said anything. Perhaps he decided that beer is more important than virginity.

B.V., OR BEFORE Vibrators

It seems that in the ancient days women often inserted strange objects where they didn't belong. An old Navajo myth tells about the time that the first women and the first men had a fight, and all the men moved to the other side of the river, leaving the women all alone. Eventually, goes the tale, some of the women started feeling very frustrated. Vibrators hadn't been invented yet, so instead they tried inserting various objects Down There. Among the objects they experimented with: an antelope horn, an eagle feather, a smooth, long stone, a cactus (Ouch! Don't try this at home!). As a result of their experimentation the women gave birth, not to cute fuzzy little animals that would help them invent beer, but to monsters that roamed the earth, eating people. Eventually most of the monsters would be killed by a hero named Monster-Slayer, but that's another story.

five

G. I. Janes

Maeve

Maeve, the ancient Irish queen of Connaught, was a scandal. Her name meant "drunken woman," and she behaved like one. If she'd been anyone but a queen you'd have called her a slut. She used to boast—while in her cups, no doubt—that she could exhaust thirty men in a night. Whatever the truth of the matter, it was a fact that if you wanted to be king of Connaught, you had to be married to Maeve, and she had already been married to three other kings before her latest husband, King Ailill.

Maeve, the ancient Irish queen of Connaught

One infamous night, they were lying in bed together, feeling all lovey-dovey, when Ailill made the mistake of sighing happily, "Good is the wife of a good man."

Maeve sat up and shook her long red hair back from her face. "Excuse me?" she asked. "Exactly what did you mean by that remark?"

"I only meant, m'dear, that you're a better woman today than when I married you."

"Hello? I was good before I ever met you."

Ailill was treading on dangerous ground, but he didn't know when to stop. "Oh you were, were you? That's funny, the way I heard it, until I did you the favor of marrying you, you were a mere weak woman, unable to stop the enemies at your boundaries from slaughtering your subjects."

He should never have said that. Maeve's blood rose to her face, and her voice rose, too. "It just so happens that I am a great warrior," she answered hotly, "with fifteen hundred warriors and fifteen hundred chiefs at my command.

"And as for marrying me, your own brother wanted to marry me, and I rejected him for you. No husband of mine can be stingy, or jealous, or a coward. He can't be cowardly, because I myself lead my warriors in battle; he can't be jealous, because I've always had one man in the shadow of another. And as for stingy, I'm richer than you. Just look at the fortune I gave you for a wedding gift. In fact, let's face it, you're nothing without me."

Ailill scoffed, "Richer than *moi?* I'm the richest person in Ireland, and you know it!"

By now Maeve and Ailill were furious at each other. Maeve clapped her hands and a servant came running. "Bring in everything we own," Maeve commanded. "And stack our possessions side by side. We'll see who's richer!"

For the rest of the night, servants raced back and forth, piling up the possessions of their king and queen. First came their golden plates and drinking horns, and their iron cauldrons; then their rings and bracelets and chains and brooches, and Maeve had just as many as Ailill. Then the servants brought in Maeve's and Ailill's wardrobes, and they both had the same number of velvet cloaks and silken robes and hand-knit fisherman sweaters. Then in came the animals, and soon the bedroom was filled with sheep and horses and pigs, bleating and oinking and trampling all over the bed, and for every

prize ram that Maeve owned, Ailill owned one just as good. By now it was well past noon of the next day, and only the vast herds of cattle remained to be counted. Nobody had gotten any sleep, and everybody was in a bad mood. Grumpily, the servants went off to the royal fields and brought in all the cows, bulls, and calves to be counted. The cattle counting revealed that Maeve's herd was as big as Ailill's—with one exception. Ailill owned a prized white bull named Fionnbanach, the best bull in all of Connaught, and Maeve had nothing to compare with him.

Maeve was furious. She called her right-hand man, MacRoth, whom she was probably sleeping with, over to her side. "I won't be beaten by that weasel of a husband," she vowed to him. "Do you know of any bull, anywhere in all Ireland, that is as great as Fionnbanach?"

"There is one," answered MacRoth, "who is twice as good, and that's the Brown Bull of Cuailgne. But he's owned by Daire, the king of Cuailgne."

"Then take nine of my best men and go to Cuailgne," ordered Maeve. "And ask Daire for the loan of his prize bull, and I'll return him after a year along with fifty cows as interest. And tell him that if his subjects think badly of him for sending away the greatest bull in all of Ireland, he should come along with the bull, and I'll build him his own palace next to ours, and give him a golden chariot to ride in. Plus I'll give him the friendship of my thighs."

It was that line about the friendship of her thighs that sold Daire when he heard it, and he got so excited that he bounced up and down on his throne until the cushions burst. "No problem," he said. "I'll send the bull back with you tomorrow, and I'll come along myself." He was already anticipating Maeve's thighs.

Then Daire ordered a feast to be spread for MacRoth and his men, and he was so delighted that he insisted on an entire roasted boar accompanied by the best of everything, including ale—lots of ale— and Maeve's men got drunk and loose-lipped. Loose lips, of course, sink ships, and by the end of the night Maeve's ship was sunk, when one of Maeve's men casually remarked, "Hey, it's lucky for Daire that he's lending his bull to our queen, because if he had refused, she just would have taken it, anyway."

That did it! The next day, Daire sent them on their way, without the bull. "And it's a good thing," roared Daire, "that I'm not in the habit of beheading messengers or not one of you would return to Connaught alive. Now get out before I change my mind!"

"Well darn!" exclaimed Maeve, when her men returned empty-handed. "We'll just have to fight for that bull!"

So Maeve called out thirty hundred armed men from the east of her land and thirty hundred armed men from the west of her land, and rode ahead of them in her chariot, leading Connaught in a war against the rest of Ireland, and all because of a brown bull. Not only was she a fierce warrior, but Maeve suffered from the worst PMS in the world; all fighting had to stop while she had her periods.

Maeve and Ailill eventually lost the war, even though they managed to capture the bull. Fat lot of good it did them anyway, because as soon as the brown bull and the white bull met face to face, they battled and didn't stop until they had killed each other. Their personalities were a lot like Maeve's.

Maeve's GRAVE

Outside of Sligo in Ireland stands a tall hill called Knocknarea. White pebbles and small white rocks lie scattered at the foot of the hill. Traditionally, those who want to climb Knocknarea must carry a white stone up with them and leave it at the top. The hill is a cairn, an ancient Irish burial mound. It will never be excavated, because it's also tradition that Maeve, the greatest, most scandalous warrior queen of Ireland, is buried there, and no one would dream of disturbing her resting place. She might get mad!

The Morrigan

The Tuatha De Danaan were a rowdy bunch of ancient Irish deities who enjoyed drinking, loving, and fighting. Their leader in battle was their brawling queen, the Morrigan, who took the shape sometimes of a hag and sometimes a raven, but most often as a wild and beautiful red-haired woman. The Morrigan had nothing against an occasional fling with a well-buffed mortal, and loved to join in any fight, private or otherwise. One day she caught a glimpse of the famous hero of Ulster, Cuchulain, who was single-handedly taking on the entire army of the kingdom of Connaught. It didn't matter to her that this Irish superhero, for all his rock star looks, was intellectually challenged. After all, she wasn't planning to spend the night with him discussing Yeats and the Celtic Revival. "Now there's a man who looks like he knows how to have a good time," she murmured.

Before dawn the next day, Cuchulain was awakened by a terrible racket. He emerged from his tent, bellowing, "Could you keep it down? I have to fight in the morning." Then he stopped, mouth open in amazement. A total stunner stood before him dressed in filmy scarlet garments, her copper-colored hair falling to her knees. Behind her, a red horse pulled a cart loaded down with gleaming gold, and behind the horse milled a mooing herd of red cows, as far as the eye could see. The girl looked up at Cuchulain through long lashes and pouted prettily.

"Top o' the morning to ye, Cuchulain," she breathed. "I'm a teenage princess and president of your fan club, and I've brought you all of daddy's gold and cattle to help you win the war."

Cuchulain, however, was a fighter, not a lover, so he sneered, "I'm not needin' the help of no colleen! I can fight me own battles."

The beautiful redhead put her hands on her hips and squinted at him. "Well if ye won't have me as yer girlfriend, ye'll have me as yer enemy. And beating me will be harder than getting through *Finnegan's Wake!*" And with that, she turned into a raven and flew up to the highest bough of a tree.

At that point Cuchulain realized his strange visitor was the Morrigan, and he was furious. He yelled up, "Arragh! And I shoulda known it was yerself! Well, ye'll not be beatin' me!" There's nothing the Irish like better than a good shouting match.

Cuchulain crawled back into his tent and tried to get some sleep. The next day his enemies sent their greatest champion against him. As the two men fought beside the river, the Morrigan, in the shape of a red cow, led her herd of cattle into the water, and they muddied it so that Cuchulain found himself slipping and sliding in the mire. With one mighty thrust of his shillelagh, Cuchulain, never much of an animal rights person, broke the red cow's leg. The Morrigan was forced to limp off, leading the herd with her, and he won that day's battle.

The Morrigan

The next morning, the Morrigan took the form of an eel, winding around Cuchulain's feet and tripping him up as he fought in the running water. He stomped with all his strength on the slippery thing, and as it wriggled away, its ribs were crushed. Cuchulain won that day's battle, too.

Finally, the Morrigan took the shape of a snarling wolf who seized Cuchulain's good right spear arm in her pointy teeth. With his left hand, the Irish hero picked up a huge rock and put out the wolf's eye. Blinded, the animal staggered away, and Cuchulain won again. But fighting for three straight days had wiped him out. He dragged himself back to his tent, thinking, "This is thirsty work." And just as he added to himself, "What wouldn't I give for a pint of Guinness?" he saw before him—not a pub, but an old, lame, half-blind woman milking a red cow. You'd think that by now Cuchulain would have learned that red cows are not what they seem, but nobody ever said he had any muscles in his head, so he went up to the woman and asked for some milk.

"Cushlamachree, wouldn't I give you some milk gladly, mavourneen," she replied, "if ye'll give me your blessing in return." And with that she handed him a creamy goblet of white milk. Cuchulain downed it in one gulp and wiped off the milk mustache. "My thanks, and good health to the giver," he declared, and the old woman's ribs were healed. She refilled the goblet and he drank it down again, adding, "My thanks, and good health to the giver." This time the crone's leg was made whole again. She poured out one more goblet full of milk, and watched keenly as the dimwitted hero finished it. As soon as he repeated, "My thanks, and good health to the giver," her eye was healed. She turned back into a raven and flew up to the highest branch of a tree.

Cuchulain realized he'd been tricked. (It wasn't hard to do!) He shook his fist at the bird who perched high above, laughing at him. "Faith and begorra," he yelled, "had I known it was you, I'd not have done it!"

But the Morrigan circled his head three times and flew away.

THE FIGHTING *Irish?*

Not all the Irish goddesses were warlike. The Morrigan's beautiful sister, Brigit, spent most of her time tending her herd of magic red cows—yes, red again. Brigit was the goddess of poetry and healing, and wells were sacred to her. The ancient Irish loved her so much that even when Saint Patrick and his fellow monks arrived to convert everybody to Christianity, the people refused to give her up. Under the theory that if you can't lick 'em, you should join 'em, the Catholic Church turned the goddess

Saint Brigid

into Saint Brigid, and said that she had nursed the Baby Jesus. All throughout the Celtic lands you'll find places called Brideswell, or Bridwell. These are all named after Brigit, the goddess who survived Christianity.

Oya

When the African people were taken in chains to the New World as slaves, their gods followed them and mixed with their European captors' Christianity to form new religions. In Haiti the new religion was called Voudoun, in Brazil it was Macumba, and in Cuba, where the Yoruba people of Nigeria were brought, it was Santéria. The Santéria gods are called orishas, and are divided into two groups. The white orishas, such as Orisha-Oko, god of farming, or Oshun, goddess of love, have powers of life. On the other hand, you get three guesses about the specialties of the dark orishas.

Oya, owner of storms and guardian of the cemetery

The fierce and beautiful warrior Oya, owner of storms and guardian of the cemetery, is—surprise!—one of the dark orishas. Her husband Chango is the orisha of thunder and lightning, so of course the two warriors fight side by side, causing tempests and terrifying thunderstorms.

Oya and Chango weren't always evenly matched. Chango was the stronger of the two, because he could breathe fire from his nose and mouth. Oya really resented this. She was very beautiful, and Chango had chosen her above sixteen other goddesses who all vied for his affections, and she was very strong, for what is stronger than the wind? Yet despite her beauty and strength, Chango had no intention of sharing his power, so, as always seems to be the case, Oya had to steal it.

Once Chango was being pursued through the forest by a whole army of enemies, all determined to do him in. Out of breath, bruised, and bleeding, the handsome orisha just managed to make it to his house in a small clearing before his enemies got there. He pounded on the door until Oya let him in.

With hands on hips, she cocked her head and frowned at him. "Look at you, you're a mess. What's the trouble this time, another woman?"

Chango was embarrassed, because it was all about a woman. With Chango, it was always about a woman. But he said, "Does it matter? There's about a thousand people out there, and they're after my hide. I could use some help, if you don't mind."

Oya was used to Chango's skirt-chasing, and she usually didn't mind, especially because it always got him into trouble, which served him right. She thought for a moment and then said, "I have a plan. What we'll do is, we'll switch identities. I'll disguise myself as you, and you'll dress up as me. We'll confound them."

Oya's usual outfit consisted of nine colorful skirts, each one worn over the other, forming a wide crinoline effect, and nine brightly colored scarves wound around her head. These she put on Chango. Then she stepped back and surveyed the effect, trying not to laugh at his discomfort. "You wouldn't fool anybody close up," she said, "but from far away, they'll recognize my clothes and think it's me. You need one more thing." She then cut off her thick black hair and glued it on Chango's head so that he had her luxurious curling locks. She saved just a little of it, which she glued to her own chin, and now she had a beard just like Chango.

Chango looked at himself in a mirror. "I feel ridiculous in this getup," he grumbled, "but it just might work."

By now they could hear Chango's pursuers breaking noisily through the underbrush and surrounding the house. They yelled through the window, "We know you're in there, Chango! Come on out so we can kill you!"

Clumsily knocking chairs over with his wide skirts, Chango made his way to his room. "There's one last thing I must do," he announced. "Then I'll be ready."

Oya knew what he was going to do; he was going to make the magic that allowed him to breathe flames from his nose and mouth. He jealously guarded the secret of this magic from Oya, and she never pushed. This time, however, she suggested, "You know, Chango, we'd have twice the power over your enemies if I could breathe fire, too."

"It'll be a cold day in hell," said Chango. "Pigs will fly. In other words, don't even think about it." And he shut his door.

Then Oya did something she had never done before: she spied on Chango through the keyhole of his locked door. She saw him take a golden key from a chain around his neck and unlock a brass chest. From the chest he brought out a small green glass bottle that shone like an emerald in the sunbeams that came through the window. He uncorked it and downed the contents. When he replaced the bottle, small sparks had already started escaping from his nostrils.

"So that's his secret," Oya murmured to herself. By the time Chango emerged from his room, she was standing at the other end of the house, energetically stirring up a gumbo on the stove and humming to herself. She gave Chango a big hug and kiss for luck, and while they were kissing, she secretly stole the key from around his neck.

Then she watched from the window as Chango stepped out the front door, and, imitating Oya's majestic walk, calmly marched past his enemies, holding the nine skirts up out of the dirt. They had no quarrel with Oya, in fact, they feared and respected her, so they tipped their hats politely as Chango passed.

Oya wasted no time unlocking the brass chest in Chango's room. She removed the green glass bottle and held it up to the light. There was still some liquid left in the bottom! Raising it to her lips, she drained every drop. Instantly, Oya felt fire surging through her. She raced back to the front door and pulled it open. Outside, Chango had already turned upon his pursuers, flames emerging from his nose and mouth, lightning flashing from his fingertips. His enemies panicked. They didn't know what to make of it. "Oya has Chango's powers!" they screamed. "We're lost!" They stampeded back toward the house, crushing those who fell beneath their feet, only to be met at the door by Oya in her Chango disguise. And she too breathed fire! By now they were hopelessly confused and despairing. "And there's Chango," they cried, "looking like Oya! They've traded bodies!" They knew they were doomed.

Oya and Chango stood back to back and obliterated the enemy with their combined strength of thunder, lightning, and tornado-force winds. Not until everyone had either fled or been killed did Chango turn to Oya and exclaim, "Woman, you stole my powers!"

Oya grinned. "And I used them well, didn't I?"

Of course, once Oya had Chango's powers, she wasn't about to give them up. Now they battle side by side, both breathing fire. But Oya has a fierce temper and Chango has a roving eye, so sometimes they fight each other, and those are the fiercest storms, where hurricane winds howl and people cower inside and pray for the orishas to kiss and make up.

WHAT'S THIS ABOUT THE *Cemetery?*

When she's not being a warrior, Oya is owner of the cemetery. She used to be owner of the seas, and it was the orisha Yemaya who owned the cemeteries. Tired of her depressing queendom, Yemaya hatched a plot. Walking with Oya one day, she steered her to the cemetery walls. The walls were high and imposing, the gate featured winged cherubs carved from marble, and you couldn't see the graves inside. You could only see the tops of the tallest statues.

"These are the walls of my fabulous mansion," she told Oya. "I have a private gym, a Jacuzzi, two swimming pools, and works of art imported from all over the world. Look, you can just see the tops of my statues from ancient Rome."

"Wow!" Oya was impressed. "All I have is water—endless water. It really gets boring."

Yemaya acted casual. "You know, I'm tired of my butlers and maids and marble halls. I might be willing to trade my property for yours."

Oya was thrilled. "Done!" she exclaimed. "The seas are yours, and you can have them!"

But the minute she walked in through the ornate gates and saw row upon row of graves, Oya realized she had been tricked. It was too late, the trade had been made, and Yemaya was already out there frolicking with the dolphins. Oya never forgave Yemaya for tricking her, and the two are still enemies. Oya eventually accepted her responsibility as guardian of the cemetery, and today she's the only orisha who's on speaking terms with Death and doesn't fear him.

six

Goddesses Who Love Too Much

Kannaki

Kannaki, who lived in second-century India, was one of those women who can be a perfect bitch to the rest of the world, but who turn into a perfect doormat for some no-account guy. Her husband, Kovalan, was as no-account as they get. He dumped Kannaki for a dancing girl and threw away his entire fortune on the hussy, but his wife was sappy enough to take him back when he came crawling to her with empty pockets.

"It's okay," she consoled him. "I still have two fabulously expensive ankle bracelets made of gold and filled with rubies. You can sell one of them and get enough money for us to open a small mom-and-pop corner grocery."

The couple then set out for the city of Madura, which had a big market. A kindly old woman named Madari let them stay in her cottage right outside of the city, and there Kannaki waited while Kovalan headed for the market with the golden ankle bracelet. The poor guy was such a loser that he didn't even notice the white bull that crossed his path. If he had, he'd have recognized it as a very bad omen and returned straightway to the cowherd's hut. Instead he headed for the market and approached a goldsmith.

Holding out his wife's bangle, he asked, "Pardon me, but perhaps you might give me an idea of how much I could get for this piece of jewelry?"

This particular goldsmith was the worst person Kovalan could have approached. The goldsmith actually was a thief, who had just stolen the queen's gold ankle bracelet. When he saw Kovalan cluelessly holding out a bangle that looked exactly the same as the one he'd just stolen, he got an idea. "I can tell the king that this is the stolen bracelet," he told himself. "This poor sap will take the rap, and I'll get away with the bracelet, and maybe even get a reward!"

To Kovalan, he said, "This ankle bracelet is fit for the queen. You just wait here in my hut, and I'll take it to the king for you, and bring back lots of money."

So while the unsuspecting Kovalan sat in the gold-smith's lean-to, the thief went straight to the king. He prostrated himself before the throne and held up the bangle. "Your

Kannaki

Highness, here's the ankle bracelet stolen from the queen this very morning, and it just so happens that I have the thief waiting at my hut in the marketplace."

The enraged king sent four of his strongest soldiers armed with razor-sharp swords to the goldsmith's hut, with orders to separate Kovalan's neck from his shoulders. Which they did.

Meanwhile, faithful Kannaki had been patiently awaiting her husband in the cowherd's cottage, when she saw Madari, the old woman, approaching. Madari looked seriously upset. She had already heard the news of Kovalan's execution, and was trying to figure out how to break the news to Kannaki.

"What's wrong?" asked Kannaki. "You look terrible! Something's wrong, isn't it? Is it my husband? He hasn't run off with another dancing girl, has he?"

Madari stuttered, "Nothing's wrong—well, yes, actually, something is wrong. Sit down. Would you like some tea? Water? No? Remember your husband? Well, there's been an accident, and he's hurt—actually, he's dead. The king had him executed for stealing the queen's bangle."

Kannaki was grief-stricken, but her anger at this great injustice was even greater than her grief. She marched out of the hut and didn't stop until she arrived at the palace gates. The palace guard took one look at her and ran to the king. "Your Highness, there's a beautiful but furious woman at the gates, demanding to see you. If I didn't know better, I'd say it was the goddess Kali herself!"

The king had her escorted to his throne, where he lounged, eating grapes and being fanned by dancing girls. Kannaki didn't waste any time. "I have something to say to you, your idiotic majesty. You had my husband wrongly killed for a crime he didn't commit, and I can prove it. That ankle bracelet was mine, and if you break it open, you'll see. My bangle is filled with rubies."

"Hmmm," mused the king. "The queen's bangle is filled with pearls." And he commanded that the ankle bracelet be brought to him. He pried it open, and immediately a ruby flew into his face.

The king was so horrified when he realized what he had done that he collapsed and died of remorse on the spot. But this was not enough for Kannaki. Maddened by grief and rage, she wanted to punish the entire city of Madura. With superhuman strength born of fury, she twisted off her own left breast. (Warning: Do not try this, at home or anywhere!) Holding up the breast, she circled the city three times, cursing it, then she hurled the breast into the street. Instantly the god of fire, with blue skin and hair red as flames, rose from the breast. He bowed to Kannaki.

"O great wronged lady, what is your request?"

"Destroy this city by fire," she answered. "Spare only the holy cows, the priests, the old people and the children, and virtuous women, but don't spare the dancing girls."

At this the four gods of Madura left the city and withdrew their protection. Flames sprang up everywhere, but didn't go near the cows, the priest or old people, or the homes of good women and their children. The dancing girls, on the other hand, watched in dismay as their theater was destroyed by fire and they shouted, "Excuse me, but who is this person? Who died and made her king?" (They didn't know that the king had indeed died.) "She's just jealous because we're prettier than her and we've been trained in the sixty-four arts of dancing and flute playing and lovemaking, and she hasn't!"

That was all they had a chance to say before the flames reached them. Soon the dead king, along with his queen, his dancing girls, his palaces, armies, and elephants, along with the thieves and bad people of the city, were reduced to ashes. As for Kannaki, she climbed a sacred mountain that lay fourteen day's walk from the burned city of Madura. Once on the top, she seated herself in a flowery grove and meditated until Indra, lord of the gods, came down and brought her back up to heaven with him. There all the deities were waiting for her, and they turned her into a goddess.

We hope she got her breast back.

Divine SELF-MUTILATION

Very rarely do dieties seem to go in for self-mutilation, and even then, they seem to be mostly males. The Irish god Nuada lost an arm in battle and had a silver one made. Thereafter he was known as Nuada of the Silver Arm. The Welsh god, Bran the Blessed, mortally wounded by a poison spear, instructed his companions to cut off his head. They obeyed him and sailed with the head to the hill where the Tower of London now stands, where they stayed for eighty years, while Bran's head stayed fresh and whole, entertaining them with pleasant stories and songs.

Still, Nuada didn't choose to lose his arm, and Bran was a goner anyway, having been poisoned. The Norse god Odin, on the other hand, plucked out his own eyeball and traded it to the Norn maidens in return for a drink from the well of wisdom, which they guarded.

However, the title of Divine Self-Mutilation Queen goes to the Christian martyr, Saint Lucy, who did Odin one better. As is usual with female

saints, Lucy had vowed to remain a virgin, so she rejected all her suitors. Because she was one of the stunners of the ancient world, all the guys wanted to love Lucy. Finally, when she'd explained for the umpteenth time to one of her suitors that she was saving herself for Jesus, he objected, "But you have such beautiful eyes." At that, Lucy plucked out both her eyes and handed them to him on a plate, saying, "You like my eyes? Here, take them." (And no matter how religious you are, don't do this at home!) Whereupon her horrified father had her put to death.

For the most part, though, you won't find much self-mutilation among female immortals. Women just don't like to spoil their looks. On the other hand, they often seem to require it of their worshipers (*See* page 169, sidebar).

Circe

There were no support groups for Women Who Love Too Much back in ancient Greece, which is too bad, because the sorceress Circe could have used one. She was definitely addicted to love, always falling for the wrong kind of guy. But when she got dumped, she got even.

It's no surprise that Circe was the way she was, since she came from a very dysfunctional family. Her father was Helios, who drove Apollo's chariot of the sun around the sky all day, which means his kids never saw him. He left for work before they woke up, and didn't get home until they were asleep. As for Circe's sister, Pasiphae, she was the infamous queen who got the hots for a bull, and had to climb inside a cow dummy in order to consummate the affair. The result of this weird mating was the minotaur, a half-man, half-bull monster that Pasiphae's hubby, King Minos, kept hidden in a labyrinth beneath their palace. Don't even ask what Pasiphae's labor must have been like!

Circe had been a queen too, but when the king, her husband, died under suspicious circumstances, she moved to Aeaea, a small island in the Mediterranean, to avoid accusations of poisoning. There she built herself a modest little palace in the middle of the island, and passed her days in the kitchen, stirring up concoctions in a big iron cauldron. This lady loved to cook!

One day a hunky guy named Glaucus pulled his rowboat up on her shore. A gal gets lonely on an island with nothing for company but toads and poison mushrooms, and Glaucus had the face of—well, of a Greek god. Circe eyed the rippling muscles beneath his scanty tunic and breathed, "Do stay for dinner."

She whipped up a little five-course dinner with two different wines, and for dessert, she changed into something more comfortable, which in Circe's case, happened to be her own bare skin. Glaucus turned pale and stammered, "I'm, um, really flattered, Circe, and, um, under any other circumstances, er, but I happen to be in love with a nymph named Scylla, who is slimmer than you and has bigger breasts, and the reason I came to you was to get a potion to make her love me."

Circe managed to control herself, only just. She took a deep breath and said, "That's quite all right, ha ha, I don't mind being rejected. Now, as for this Scylla, why don't you tell me where the slu—er, young lady swims, and I'll sprinkle a little something in the water for her."

And sprinkle a little something is what she did, only it was a little something that turned Scylla into a hideous monster.

The next man to break Circe's heart was a minor god named Pictus, who spurned her for a goddess named Pomona. Circe slipped him a mickey, and while watching him turn into a woodpecker, she got her inspiration. "All men are beasts!" she declared, "so that's what I'll do—I'll turn them into beasts!"

After that, Circe tried out her brews on any hapless sailors who washed up on her island. She would treat them to her unique hospitality: a good meal followed by spiked wine that turned them into lions and tigers and bears, oh my. Pretty soon the place was a zoo, literally. One day the Greek hero Odysseus, on his way home from the Trojan War, landed on her island with all his men. As soon as their feet touched land, they found themselves surrounded by what should have been fierce wild beasts, but these animals gathered around the sailors like so many pussycats.

"I don't like this," said Odysseus' second in command, Eurylochus. "There's some kind of enchantment here."

"Nonsense," answered Odysseus. "Don't be so paranoid. Tell you what: you take the men and explore the island, and I'll stay here and guard the ship."

Eurylochus and the sailors hadn't gone far before they came across Circe's marble palace, and the sorceress herself was there to meet them at her front door, clad in a filmy little tunic with an apron over it and a wooden spoon in her hand. "Welcome to my humble island," she said. "You must be hungry."

The sailors poured into the dining room, all except Eurylochus the paranoid, who hung back and watched the scene through a keyhole. The sailors, who were simple men and had never learned table manners, didn't bother with knives and forks. They attacked Circe's gourmet dishes with their hands and slurped the soup from her golden bowls. Circe watched with disgust, thinking, "What pigs—say, that's an idea!"

And when the dessert wine had been guzzled down, the men felt their noses turning into snouts, their arms lengthening into front legs, and their cries of horror emerging as squeals. They had become pigs! Eurylochus, who'd witnessed it all through the keyhole, raced back to the ship.

"Quick, Odysseus," he panted, "we gotta vamoose! Some crazy chick just turned all the guys into pigs!"

But Odysseus was far too macho to let a mere woman beat him. He buckled on his sword and strode over to Circe's place. Quicker than she could say, "Won't you stay for dinner?" he had the sword pointed at her throat.

Now Circe was a bit of a masochist, and she had a weakness for guys who take control. She breathed, "My man!" and off came the tunic.

Circe

Circe changed all the sailors back to men again, and she and Odysseus lived together for a year, most of which Circe spent cooking up French cuisine for her sweetie and his crew. Then one day Odysseus told her, "Well, it's been swell, but I have to leave now and return to my wife and son."

Circe was devastated. "Y-your wife and son?" she sobbed. "You never told me!" And she would have turned him into a pig then and there, but Odysseus was too wily to drink any of her wine. He even managed to convince her to restock the ship with gourmet food (but no wine) and to give them a really good map when they left.

The heartbroken sorceress couldn't give up hope that her lover might return, and for a good six months she patrolled the shore, looking for his ship. Finally she had to face the truth. "He doesn't call, he doesn't write," she exclaimed bitterly. "That's what I get for being such a pushover."

Being the daughter of a god, Circe is probably still there on her island, experimenting with new spells and waiting for another guy to show up and try out her latest brew. She leaves women alone, but if you're a man vacationing on the Mediterranean, beware of Greek girls bearing retsina!

WHEN MEN ACT LIKE *Beasts*

Circe wasn't the only one to turn men into beasts when they deserved it. The *Mabinogian*, an ancient Welsh collection of myths, tells the story of Math Mathonwy, a wizard, and his beautiful handmaiden, Goewin. Math's nephew, Gilfaethwy, got the hots for Goewin, and with his brother Gwydion's help, he raped her. When Math found out about the rape, he first saved Goewin's reputation by marrying her himself, then he punished the brothers in a unique way. They had acted like beasts, so he struck them with his wand and they became a doe and a stag, running off into the forest for a year. Then they returned to his court along with their child, a young fawn. Math changed the fawn into a boy and adopted him. As for the brothers, he turned them into wild boars and switched their sexes; now the one who had been a stag was a sow and the doe was a male boar. A year later they returned with their little piglet child, who Math turned into a boy and adopted. A third time he changed the brothers. This time the sow became a wolf and the boar became a she-wolf, and again they returned a year later with their cub, whom Math changed into a boy and adopted into his growing group of foster sons.

Finally Math struck the animals with his wand and they were human brothers again, but they had learned what it's like to be female, and to be animals.

Izanami

Before there was a land called Japan, goes the myth, it had to be created. So an immortal couple, Izanami and Izanagi, were sent down to earth by the gods, who gave them a jeweled spear and commanded them to create life. Izanami and Izanagi looked down upon the vast ocean that was earth from the Floating Bridge of Heaven, and stirred up the waters with the magic spear. When they lifted the spear, drops of water fell from it and formed the first land. The first couple climbed down to their new home, and for the first time, Izanami took a good look at her mate, and found him to be a total stud.

"Wow, you are so hot," she exclaimed, "Let's have sex!"

Izanagi was a little annoyed, because he felt that, as the guy, it was up to him to make advances, but he also couldn't resist the invitation, especially since Izanami, with her glossy black hair rippling past her waist and the come-hither look in her lustrous dark eyes, was a knockout, so he said, "Sure!"

No sooner did they have sex than Izanami got pregnant and gave birth. Their first child was a tiny leech-creature, which swam away into the waters, and their second was a small island consisting only of foam.

"What kind of kids are these?" complained Izanagi, "We were not put on Earth to create leeches and foam. Something's wrong!" So the couple went back up the Floating Bridge of Heaven to ask the gods for help.

"You didn't do it right," explained the gods, "The man is supposed to make the advances, not the woman. Go back down and start all over again."

Izanagi exclaimed, "I knew it!" but Izanami wasn't too happy with this ruling. Nevertheless, they went back down to their island. This time, Izanagi turned to his mate and said, "Wow, you are so hot! Let's have sex," and Izanami answered, "Sure."

Now they were cooking with gas! In quick succession, Izanami gave birth to the islands that make up Japan, to the trees, mountains, rivers and winds. Next she and Izanagi begat the gods: Amaterasu the sun goddess, Susanoo the storm god, and Tsukiyomi the moon god. And despite all these births, she kept her fabulous figure! The couple thoroughly enjoyed every

Izanami

minute they spent in the begetting, until one day Izanami gave birth to Fire, and it killed her (you can just imagine!).

Izanagi was inconsolable. In a fury, he drew his sword and cut off the head of their flaming baby. Of course, you can't really kill fire, but from the drops of the baby's blood sprang eight mountains and eight more gods. Then he journeyed to the opening of the Underworld and, sobbing bitterly, he called for his mate to come out.

"Izanami, the lands we've made aren't finished. We still have a lot of begetting to do. Please come back!" Izanami heard his weeping and crept as far as the gate to the world above. She peered out and called out softly to him, but stayed in the shadows so her mate couldn't see her.

"I wish you'd come earlier," she told him, "I've already eaten the food of the dead, and I don't think I can return to the living world now."

Izanagi pleaded, "But, beautiful Izanami, my love, I can't live without you! No other woman could ever take your place! I'll love you and only you until eternity!"

Izanami was touched. "Okay, I'll go to the Lord of the Dead for permission. But you have to wait here for me. Don't come down to the Underworld, and whatever you do, don't look at me!"

"Whatever. But hurry!"

So Izanagi waited for his beloved mate at the door to the Underworld.

And waited.

And waited.

Eventually he grew impatient. "Women!" he fretted, "They take so long to get ready. She's probably doing her hair, deciding what kimono to wear, trying on shoes. I'll go get her."

He took a wooden comb from his hair and lighted it on fire, then, holding it high like a torch, descended into the dark tunnel to the Underworld. Soon he saw the shadowy form of his dead mate up ahead of him. He walked faster, and caught up with her. Izanami heard his footsteps behind her and turned around. By torchlight, Izanagi saw his wife for the first time since she had died.

She was disgusting! Maggots crawled in and out of her eye sockets. Gobbets of putrid flesh fell from her body. Her nose was eaten away! What had he expected?

Izanagi spun on his heel and fled toward the land of the living as fast as his trembling legs could carry him. He called back, "Whoops! Look at the time, gotta run! Maybe we can do lunch sometime, but don't call me, I'll call you!"

Izanami was furious. "I told you not to look! Now you've shamed me in front of all the dead!" And she gave chase, accompanied by her girl-demons, the Ugly Girls from Hell. Izanagi ripped a second comb from his hair and tossed it behind him, where it turned into a bunch of grapes. Izanami skidded to a stop. "Food from the Land of the Living!" she exclaimed, stuffing the grapes into her mouth and sharing them with her demon followers.

Izanagi sped on, breathing hard, hoping that the grapes had stopped her, but when he turned to look, she was gaining on him again, bits of decaying flesh dropping behind her as she ran. She held out her bony arms to him, and two fingers dropped off. "Come back here, honey buns, and give your sweetie a big kiss! You promised to love me forever!"

Yeah, right. Izanagi plucked an ornament out of his fancy headdress and tossed that behind him. It turned into bamboo shoots, and Izanami and her girl-demons paused long enough to gobble them up, then continued their pursuit. As Izanami chased her fleeing lover, she shouted, "Fourflusher! You said you couldn't live without me! Come back with me then, to the Land of the Dead! After a while you won't notice the smell anymore!" But Izanagi ran like the wind, pausing only long enough to rip another ornament from his hair and toss it behind him, where it became peaches and stopped Izanami and her demon-girls only for a minute.

Finally, in desperation, Izanagi grabbed a humongous rock that would take a thousand men to lift. He rolled it into the path between himself and his rotting true-love. Izanami was furious. She couldn't climb the rock, or squeeze herself around it. She leaned across it as far as she could reach and screamed at Izanagi, "You rat! You promised eternal love, and now you've changed your mind just because of a few lousy maggots! I'll teach you to be fickle! Every day I'll steal the souls of a thousand people from the Land of the Living."

"So what? Big deal," answered Izanagi, "Every day I'll cause fifteen hundred new people to be born."

Then Izanagi jumped into a stream to wash off the smell of decay, while the broken-hearted and rotting Izanami tottered sadly back to the Land of the Dead, where she now reigns as queen.

Women WHO Return FROM THE Dead

No matter what the place of origin, all myths seems to agree on one thing: there's no returning alive from the land of the dead. Inanna managed, but only by sending someone else down in her place. Sometimes the hero is allowed to come back up for Spring Break or Summer vacation, as is the case of Dumuzi, and the Greek Goddess Persephone. But Persephone, like Izanami, made the mistake of eating something while she was in the underworld, and even though it was just a couple of pomegranate seeds, she had to return and be queen of the Land of the Dead for six months out of every year.

Sometimes guys go down there in an attempt to bring back their dead sweethearts, but it never works. The Greek hero Orpheus, like Izanagi, descended into the Underworld hoping to get back his beloved but dead Eurydice, and actually was at the point of leading her out. But Eurydice had told him, "Don't look back at me," and Orpheus just couldn't resist sneaking a peek over his shoulder to make sure she was still following him. As soon as he did that, he broke the laws of the Underworld and lost her forever. Like Orpheus, Izanagi didn't pay attention when told not to peek, and you see what happened!

seven

They Got Away
with Murder!

Artemis

The Greek goddess Artemis was not like all those other goddesses with their handsome but often faithless mortal boyfriends. She preferred girls, and it's no wonder, when you consider the men in her family. Her own father, Zeus, king of the gods, was the ultimate Dirty Old Man. Thousands of years old, there he was sneaking around on Earth, trying—and usually succeeding—to seduce some young mortal babe. Being married to Hera, mother of the gods, didn't stop him. In his attempts to reach first base with some new hot number, he would take on strange forms, such as a swan or a shower of gold. You don't want to know exactly what these ancient Greek maidens did with swans and gold coins, but it seems to have worked for Zeus. When he got the hots for Callisto, a nymph who hung with Artemis, he actually disguised himself as Artemis in order to get it on with her. And he succeeded so well that he got Callisto in a family way.

The fact that Callisto's behavior with someone she thought was Artemis resulted in her becoming preggers tells you all you need to know about the sex lives of Artemis and her girlfriends.

As for Artemis' twin brother, the sun god Apollo, he was one of those men who don't understand the meaning of the word No. He fixated on the nymph Daphne and wouldn't leave her alone even when she told him to get lost. Finally, terrified by her obsessive stalker, she tried to escape, but Apollo chased her. Being a god, he was faster than she, and she actually had to turn herself into a tree to avoid being raped. Today a guy like that would have been slapped with a restraining order faster than you can say, "Sexual harassment," but in those days he was worshiped. Of course it helped that he was a poet and a musician with a classic Greek profile and a head of golden curls; women can't seem to resist musicians.

Artemis, on the other hand, cared little for music—except maybe the Indigo Girls—or poetry—except maybe Sappho—or any of that sissy stuff. She was goddess of the moon, and also goddess of the hunt, and for all her golden hair and the crescent moon she wore on her forehead, she was one macha chick. When she wasn't working out at the Women's Olympics Training center or leading the annual Gay/Lesbian/Bisexual/Transgender Parade, her idea of a good time was roaming the forest with her bow and arrow, killing things. The idea of shooting Bambi and cute little lop-eared bunnies didn't bother her a bit. In fact, the idea of killing people didn't even bother her!

When she discovered Callisto had become a single mother, the angry goddess felt betrayed. She turned the poor nymph and her baby son into bears and used them for target practice. Luckily, Zeus did the right thing for a change, and lifted the two bears into the heavens, where they became the Great Bear and the Little Bear, Ursa Major and Ursa Minor.

But it was men who really infuriated Artemis. She wanted nothing to do with the sweaty, hairy, loud, annoying creatures. Too bad if one of them got in her way!

One day a prince named Actaeon, who happened to be a pretty good hunter himself, was out in the forest with his hounds, looking for something to kill. As he roamed beneath the trees, girlish giggles reached his ears. It was either a very effemi-nate bear, or—"Girls!" he exclaimed. "There are girls in the woods!" And he followed the sound, leaving his dogs behind.

The Great Bear (Ursa Major) and the Little Bear (Ursa Minor)

Soon he came to a clearing and a small lake, where Artemis and her nymphs cavorted, bathing nude under the waterfall, splashing in the water and playing The Love That Dare Not Speak Its Name on the soft grass.

The nymphs, like Artemis, were all totally buffed from hours of working out at the gym, and Actaeon was one of those guys who get turned on by girls who love girls. He hid behind some bushes and watched. During a lull in the giggling, Artemis heard heavy breathing coming from behind the bushes. A wave of her hand caused the underbrush to magically part and expose

Greek nymphs

Actaeon crouched there, watching the action. The wretched prince realized for the first time that he'd been spying on a goddess, and he tried to stammer an apology. "I'm really, *really* sorry. I just got here, haven't seen a thing, honest, and anyway I promise not to tell...."

Artemis wasn't having any. She stood tall with her hands clenched into fists at her side and her voice was like ice when she spoke. "I don't like men anyway. But if there's anything I hate, it's a peeping tom." And she snapped her fingers.

Suddenly the prince felt his body changing. His arms lengthened into front legs, and his legs grew longer and thinner. Horns sprouted from his forehead. Artemis had turned him into a stag! That was when his hounds caught up with him.

"Rover!" called Actaeon, "Champ! Good boys! Down boys, heel!" But, coming from a stag, the commands didn't work the way they should, and the unfortunate ex-prince bounded away with his dogs in hot pursuit. According to the myths, Actaeon's hounds tore him to bits, but Artemis didn't care. She turned to her current favorite nymph, shrugged her shoulders, and growled, "He shouldn't have started with me. You know how I get."

Ballbusters

Artemis wasn't the only goddess who was hard on men. The Turkish goddess Cybele was even worse. Although most goddesses of the ancient world enjoyed sex with men—in fact, in the case of Ishtar/Inanna, sex was a temple sacrament—Cybele's unfortunate male worshipers worked themselves up into a frenzy and castrated themselves, throwing their severed members at the feet of their goddess. After this, they were allowed to dress up in women's clothing, paint their faces, and serve the goddess in her temple—an ancient and imperfect version of today's sex change operations.

The Aztec goddess Coatlicue was another one to avoid if you happened to be a guy. She wore a necklace of skulls, like Kali, and a skirt made from the severed penises of her castrated lovers.

Grizzly Woman

Storytellers of the Northwest Indian tribes used to tell tales of Grizzly Woman. As her name implies, she was a giant grizzly bear with magic powers and an appetite for human flesh. Once she insinuated herself into a village by marrying the chief. Her husband—and the rest of the tribe—seemed unaware that she was a bear. Probably she'd killed and eaten the chief's real wife, and was wearing the dead woman's skin: Grizzly Woman had tried that before, and almost gotten away with it.

The great bear-woman was ravenous—she was *always* ravenous—and she formed a plan to eat all the women of the village. She picked berries, five basketsful of berries, and showed them to the women. They were impressed. "Where did you get all those berries?" they asked

"Over on that island there," answered Grizzly Woman. "I can take a canoe-load of you tomorrow morning. We'll pick all the berries we want."

The next morning, Grizzly Woman loaded a canoe with twenty women and rowed them to the island. There were indeed tons of berries on the island and the women picked and ate to their heart's content. But when they got ready to leave, Grizzly Woman said, "It's getting late and I'm tired. Let's sleep here on the island, and tomorrow we can pick even more berries."

The women lay down around a campfire. Grizzly Woman sang them a magic spell that put them to sleep. Then she killed them all, eating as many as she could and stashing the extras away for later.

The next day she rowed back to the village with ten baskets-ful of berries. "Look what the women sent you!" she told them. "They're still on the island, picking berries. If you'd like, I can take a group of you there tomorrow."

This sounded great to the women, as the berries were ripe and sweet and juicy, so Grizzly Woman piled another twenty women into a canoe and rowed them to the island. Naturally when they reached the island the first batch of women were missing because she'd eaten them all, but Grizzly Woman explained, "Oh, they're on another part of the island where there

Grizzly Woman

are even more berries. Why don't you start picking berries here, and I'll be right back."

Leaving the women to fill their baskets with berries, Grizzly Woman raced to the other side of the island, where she sang at the top of her lungs. Then she raced back again. "The other women are having a great time on the other side of the island. They're so happy that they're singing. Didn't you hear them?"

To keep the women happy and clueless, Grizzly Woman started a singalong. Soon she had the women singing "Michael, Row the Boat Ashore" and "Hava Nagila" as they picked berries. Then she ran back to the other side of the island, where she sang "Kumbaya" as loud as she could, so everyone would think it was the other women. She spent the day running back and forth on the island, leading singalongs and filling in for the dead women. By the time the sun set, she didn't have to lie about being tired. She stayed awake just long enough to kill the women and eat as many as her stomach would hold. Then she stashed the leftovers away for later.

A third time Grizzly Woman rowed back to the village alone, bringing with her a dozen basketsful of berries. The remaining women gathered around and stuffed their cheeks with the ripe fruit. A little girl named Waterbug spoke up. "But where are all the women you took to the island?"

Grizzly Woman didn't like Waterbug; the kid was too smart.

In fact, she was named Waterbug after a water insect that could stay very still and then suddenly bite. But the great magical she-bear managed to grin and pat the little girl on her head. "They're still picking berries on the island. Cute kid, heh heh."

When Grizzly Woman grinned, Waterbug noticed what big, sharp, pointy teeth she had. When she patted the little girl on the head, Waterbug noticed that her hands were furry paws with long pointed claws. The other women noticed nothing; they wanted berries, and they gathered around Grizzly Woman, crying, "Take me tomorrow!" "Can I come, too?"

"And me too," added Waterbug.

Grizzly Woman said, "No, you can't come. You're too little." And she thought, "This kid spells trouble."

Waterbug wandered off, and pretended to play with her Barbies. But that night she crept into the bottom of the canoe and hid beneath a pile of baskets. Grizzly Woman didn't find her until they were almost at the island, and it was too late to turn back. "Little brat!" she raged. "You'll get in the way! Plus, you'll probably tell lies about me to all the women!"

Waterbug said nothing. She sat quietly, hugging her favorite Barbie, which she had brought with her. Once the women were ashore, Grizzly Woman set them to gathering berries. Then she excused herself "Gotta powder my nose. I'll be right back." And she ran off to the other side of the island.

Waterbug followed her. The little girl was swift and small enough to stay hidden. She watched from behind a bush when Grizzly Woman stopped in a clearing and loudly sang "Kumbaya." Then she followed the bear further, to a pile of branches. The ground all around was littered with human bones. As Waterbug watched, the bear-woman pulled up the branches and counted the bodies hidden underneath, making sure they were all there. Even someone not as smart as Waterbug would have realized what was going on.

Waterbug turned and ran as fast as she could, returning to the women before Grizzly Woman could arrive. "That's not the chief's wife, it's Grizzly Woman!" she panted. "She's already killed and eaten the other women and she means to eat us, too! But don't let on that you know, and I'll take care of it."

Just as she finished warning everybody, Grizzly Woman came lumbering through the woods. Waterbug only had time to whisper, "Act like nothing's wrong." But now the women could plainly see two furry brown ears sticking up on top of the bear-woman's head, and brown fur sticking out in places where the human skin she wore didn't quite fit together.

Grizzly Woman sensed that something was wrong. "Waterbug's been telling lies about me, hasn't she?" she demanded.

Waterbug

"Oh, no, no, *noooo*," the women assured her. But when Grizzly Woman tried to lead them in a singalong, their hearts weren't in it. Soon the sun set, and Grizzly Woman suggested they go to sleep. Waterbug had gathered clamshells on the shore, and when she lay down, she put the clamshells over her eyes, so Grizzly Woman wouldn't know that her eyes were really open. She kept her eyes open and listened as the bear-woman sang a magic spell that put all the other women to sleep.

"So that's how she does it," thought the little girl, and she memorized the song. Soon all the women were sleeping, except, of course, for Waterbug. She got up and put more wood on the fire. Grizzly Woman said, "What are you doing that for? It's too hot. Go to sleep!"

Waterbug lay down again, and pretended to sleep. After a while, Grizzly Woman very silently got up herself, and checked to make sure the women were all asleep. As she crouched over the first sleeping woman, prepared to devour her, Waterbug got up again and built up the fire.

"Jeez, will you just go to sleep? What a brat!" exclaimed Grizzly Woman, and she lay down again.

This time, Waterbug sang the magic spell she'd memorized. Grizzly Woman was pretty tired anyway, having been up half the night waiting for the kid to conk out, so no sooner did she hear the song than she was in slumberland. Quickly and silently,

Waterbug woke the other women. They tiptoed back to their canoe at the shore, and rowed away.

Unfortunately, Waterbug had never finished singing the magic song, so Grizzly Woman didn't stay asleep. As soon as she awoke, she realized that the women were escaping. Taking another canoe, she rowed after them. The women had a head start, and it looked like Grizzly woman wouldn't catch up, so she blew her nose and threw the boogers at them. This was not merely a disgusting thing to do; Grizzly Woman's snot was magic, and if it hit them, it would kill them.

All the while that she was chasing the women and trying to kill them, Grizzly Woman kept shouting, "That little brat's been telling lies about me, hasn't she? Don't listen to her, I'm your friend!"

But of course, she didn't fool anybody.

Soon the canoe carrying Waterbug and the women approached the shore of their village, with Grizzly Woman still chasing them and shouting. The chief heard the commotion, so he climbed to the top of his hut and looked out over the water. He saw the women in their canoe, and pursuing them, with tatters of human skin falling off her, a great red-eyed bear, foaming at the mouth and gnashing her sharp yellow teeth. He took a bow and arrows and shot at her.

Grizzly Woman never knew when she was licked. She

screamed up at the chief, "What, are you nuts, shooting at me? I'm your wife, idiot; don't you recognize me? That brat's been lying about me, don't believe her!"

Grizzly Woman was fast gaining on the escaping women. The chief's arrows missed her until he only had one left. In desperation, he threw the last arrow at her. She raised an arm to protect herself, and the arrow pierced her little finger. It so happened that Grizzly Woman's heart was situated in her little finger, so the arrow split her heart in two and killed her.

Many stories about Grizzly Woman end with her being killed, but she never stays dead, because nobody knows how to do it right. After all, she always returns in another story.

GETTING ON
Grizzly Woman's GOOD SIDE

Despite her insatiable appetite for human flesh, there was one way to get around Grizzly Woman. This terrifying bear-woman really liked sex. In one story, Grizzly Woman was dragging a man into her cave with the intention of killing and eating him (she had already killed and eaten his brothers), when, flailing wildly about, he accidentally grabbed her Down There. Immediately the bear-woman changed. She put the man down carefully and dusted him off. "Build up the fire," she instructed her little cub-children. "Your new father is cold. We must make him comfortable." And she kept the man alive to share her bed. We're not sure we want to imagine what sex with a bear would be like, but we can definitely say, Don't try this at home!

Kali

Kali the Destroyer, the Hindu goddess of death and destruction, wins hands-down the prize for nastiest goddess ever. The terrifying ebony-skinned goddess was born when the Hindu dieties battled an army of demons led by the demon-king, Raktabija. The problem with Raktabija was that wherever a drop of his blood was spilled, a thousand demons sprang up, so as you can imagine, things were not going well for the good guys. The gods were led into battle by Durga, the first goddess in the universe, who was no slouch herself. She was a fierce and beautiful amazon who rode on a tiger, but even she was powerless against a demon army that kept increasing. As Durga saw another thousand demon

Durga, the first goddess of the universe

warriors rise from Raktabija's spilled blood, she frowned in fury, and where her brows knitted together over her nose, Kali sprang forth, born from Durga's rage.

Kali leaped to the ground and twirled around. She was born to kill! Her blood-red lips parted in a fiendish grin. "Hello, honey," she crooned softly. "I'm *ho-ome!*"

Satisfied with her creation, Durga left the battle in Kali's competent hands—all four of them—and stepped back with the other gods to watch the action.

Kali started slowly. She had only to glare at the demons with her three crimson eyes, and half of them fell dead instantly. She then let out an earth-shattering shriek that caused even the gods to cover their ears, and more demons dropped lifeless at her feet. Laughing madly, she got down to action. She snatched up the remaining demons with her four arms and shoved them into her mouth. The demons, realizing they had met their match, tried to escape, but Kali flicked out her long red tongue and caught them as they ran, swallowing some whole and chewing the others up.

It was not until she had gobbled up the last of the fleeing demons that Kali turned her attention to Raktabija, who was nervously tiptoeing off the field of battle, hoping to escape the dark goddess' notice. Feasting on demon-flesh had made Kali even stronger, and seizing the demon-king, she lifted him into the air

Kali, the destroyer, goddess of death and destruction

as easily as you might lift a baby. She held him up for an instant, grinning into his terrified eyes. Then she said, "Yum!" and bit into his neck, drinking his blood before any could spill and turn into more demons. She drained his body and tossed it aside, while the watching gods roared out their victory cry.

But they had all underestimated Kali. She wasn't finished yet.

Kali had emerged from Durga's brow dressed in nothing but a tiger skin. Now she adorned herself. Walking among the fallen demons, she pulled them apart, fashioning a necklace and matching earrings out of their heads, and a belt made up of demon arms. Then she turned to the gods, who had been watching silently from the sidelines. As she licked some blood from her chin with her long red tongue, she struck a *Vogue* pose and asked, "Is it me?"

The gods were definitely not going to tell Kali she looked monstrous, streaked with gore and wearing severed limbs. They babbled, "Oh, it's you, it's you! Severed heads become you! Dahling, you look mahvelous!"

"That's good," Kali purred, "because a gal wants to look her best in the mosh pit." Drunk on the blood of the demon-king, her long tangled black hair falling into her face, she twirled among the dismembered corpses and began to dance. She tossed her hair back and laughed. The skulls around her neck crashed into each other and kept time like horrid castanets. She leaped upon the slain demons, stamping on their bodies, reducing them to mushy roadkill, and still she danced.

Soon the Earth itself began to quake, and the gods grew apprehensive. They looked at each other nervously. "Um, maybe it's time for someone to stop her," suggested one of the gods, but nobody volunteered. Then Shiva stepped forward. Shiva happened to be the god of the dance, so the gods figured he knew what he was talking about. "Aw, let her dance. She's only having a little fun. In fact, I'll join her."

So Shiva stepped out onto the field of corpses to dance with Kali. Unfortunately, the goddess of death and destruction was so carried away with her wild, drunken dance that she didn't even see the handsome god. Instead she executed a pirouette right into him, knocking him down, stomping and pounding upon his body.

"Hey!" Shiva called out. "Hello, you're dancing on me! Could you let me up, please?"

But Kali was deaf to the sound of anything but her own blood racing through her veins, and she continued her victory dance on Shiva's helpless body. In her frenzy she might have killed him, but luckily Kali happened to look down in mid-twirl, and she saw that she was dancing not on a demon but on the god of dance himself. Not only that, but she took one look at Shiva and realized that this god was destined to be her husband!

(Don't ask me; gods and goddesses know these things.)

Kali stopped dancing and the Earth stopped shaking. She picked up the stunned god of dance and brushed him off. "I'm *sooo* sorry, " she said. "Are you okay?"

Shiva was hardly okay. He was a mass of bruises and broken bones, but he muttered something polite and crawled away. Hard as it is to believe, the story has a happy ending, at least for Shiva and Kali. Being a mellow guy, he let bygones be bygones and married the goddess who had nearly danced him to death, although he was understandably reluctant to attend raves with her.

Kali still remains the goddess of death and destruction, and one day she'll start a dance that not even Shiva can stop, and that will be the Dance That Ends the World.

Kali's Thugs

You can see them in old movies: crazed Indian guys who strangle people with cords, chanting "Kill for the love of Kali!" They were the Thuggees, devotees of Kali, and they really existed until the mid-nineteenth century. Their murders were seen as human sacrifices to Kali, but she instructed them to kill only men, and—surprisingly for such a bloodthirsty goddess—to kill without spilling a drop of their blood. Hence the cords.

In earlier centuries, Kali wasn't quite as finicky about blood. In the 1500s, a boy's head was cut off once a week at Kali's altar in Tanjore, India. Thuggees, who gave us the word *thug*, are not to be confused with Hasheeshim, who gave us the word *assassin*. The Hasheeshim used to get stoned out of their minds on hashish, then go out and kill Christians during the Crusades. Come to think of it, the Thuggees also were probably not exactly working with drug-free minds.

Find Your Inner Bitch Goddess

I f the New Age goddess can be in your
office, in your bedroom, in the mall, in
your underwear, in your face, then cer-
tainly there can also be bits and pieces of nasty immortals
in you. The following quiz will help you find your own
special bad goddess, perhaps even several:

1. Your boyfriend dumps you for your best girlfriend. You:

   a. Wait patiently by the phone, knowing he'll call when he gets
   tired of her. While waiting, you peruse cookbooks for recipes
   for that special chocolate cake you'll bake to welcome him
   back.

   b. Tell him, "No hard feelings," and serve him that chocolate cake
   without telling him you baked it using Ex-Lax.

   c. You're disappointed, because you'd been planning to dump
   him for *her.*

2. You go home for Thanksgiving. At the dinner table, as usual, your mother asks why you're not married yet, like your sister. Your answer is to:

   a. Make drunken passes at your brother-in-law. In front of your sister.

   b. Loudly declare that you will be no man's unpaid servant, nurse, or love-slave.

   c. Ignore your mother and challenge your father to an arm-wrestling competition, just like you always do with the guys you date. Loser winds up with arm in the mashed potatoes.

3. The corner office is up for grabs. You and a coworker are both in the running to inherit it. You want out of your cubicle so badly that you are willing to:

   a. Wear your shortest, tightest dress to work and let slip to your male (or female) supervisor that you've always been fascinated by older married men (or women).

   b. Make sure that your coworker gets nothing to drink but decaf spiked with valerian for the rest of the week.

   c. Take your coworker out to a drinking lunch where you ply her with so many double martinis that she insists you're her best friend and she wants you to have to corner office. Make sure she signs a statement before she passes out.

4. You're planning a surprise party for your best friend's birthday. What kind of party do you throw?

   a. You take all the attention away from your friend by jumping out of her cake and doing an improvised dance on the table.

   b. Beer, beer, and more beer. Who needs cake?

   c. A party isn't really a party until the furniture starts getting broken and the neighbors call the cops.

Quiz over, pencils down!

1. If you answered:

   a. You are a Goddess Who Loves Too Much, specifically Kannaki. Get over it, girl; he isn't worth tearing your heart (or your breast) out!

   b. You still Love Too Much, but you're a Circe. Getting even is better than just getting mad, but we don't advocate messing around with anyone's health, even that loser of an ex. Why not just bake a chocolate cream pie and toss it in his face? As he licks the filling off, he'll remember what a good cook you were and regret dumping you for a girl who can't boil water.

   c. You are an Artemis. Go with your feelings, sister, there's a whole world of women waiting for you!

2. If you answered:

  a. Your inner goddess is Pele or maybe Inanna. The trouble is, your sister's inner goddess may be Namaka O Kahai or Ereshkigal. Don't go there.

  b. You are Lilith. Beware the demon lover.

  c. You are a warrior goddess or a warrior queen. This is cool, as long as you don't start a major war when looking for a boyfriend. And remember, the Cuchulain types usually react badly to having their arms in the mashed potatoes. Instead, look for a cute guy who backs down from challenges.

3. If you answered:

  a. You are Freya, with a little bit of Judith and even Uzume thrown in. Hey, vamping the boss could work, but keep in mind that you may be expected to deliver what you're promising.

  b. You are *such* a Circe! But be warned: Although there's a good chance that caffeine withdrawal may turn your coworker into a grouch, she may also wind up bright-eyed and rested, and able to put in a better performance than ever!

  c. You are an Inanna, or even a bit of an Isis. She's gonna be awfully mad at you in the morning! Think hard: Is the corner office worth having a bitter enemy at work?

4. If you answered:

   a. You are Uzume. You are suddenly very popular with the boys, but you just lost your best friend. Uh-oh!

   b. The spirit of Osmotar is in you. You rock, but don't make a habit of it (Can you say "Alcoholics Anonymous?"? I knew you could!) and try to put a little something in your stomach first, or you'll have a hangover tomorrow.

   c. That's the warrior queen and warrior goddess again. Better hope that your best friend didn't really value that vase before you go smashing it over someone's head!

index

bibliography

All the stories in this book are real; I have paraphrased them in my own irreverent way. For more information on these wild and woolly women, look up the following books, which take their goddesses a bit more seriously. Some of these books have been out of print so long they can only be found in your library (if you're lucky) and many are as dense as Aunt Matilda's Christmas fruitcake. But like that fruitcake, you can pick out your favorite nuts and candied fruits without having to digest the whole thing. When I have insomnia, I like to pull out my copy of Robert Graves' *The White Goddess*, open it at random, and read until it puts me to sleep.

Bolen, Jean Shinoda. *Goddesses in Everywoman*. New York: Harper Colophon Books, 1985.

Budapest, Z. *Grandmother of Time*. New York: Harper Collins, 1995, 1997.

_____ *Summoning the Fates*. New York: Three Rivers/Random House, 1998.

Eisler, Riane. *The Chalice and the Blade*. San Francisco, CA: Harper and Row, 1987.

Gimbutas, Marija. *The Goddesses and Gods of Old Europe*. Berkeley, CA: University of California Press, 1982.

_____. *The Language of the Goddess*. San Francisco, CA: Harper and Row, 1989.

_____. *The Civilization of the Goddess*. San Francisco, CA: HarperSanFrancisco, 1991.

Graves, Robert. *The White Goddess*. New York: Farrar, Strauss and Giroux, 1948.

Gregory, Lady Isabella Augusta, and W. B. Yeats, *A Treasury of Irish Myth, Legend, and Folklore*. New York: Avenel Books, 1986.

Harvey, Andrew, and Anne Baring. *The Divine Feminine*. Berkeley, CA: Conari Press, 1996.

The Kalevala. Translated by Elias Lonrot, Keith Bosley, and Albert B. Lord. Oxford: Oxford University Press, 1999.

The Mabinogian. Translated by Gwyn and Thomas Jones. The Netherlands: Dragon's Dream, 1982.

Monaghan, Patricia. *The Book of Goddesses and Heroines*. St. Paul, MI: Llewellyn Publications, 1990.

Murphy, Joseph M. *Santéria: African Spirits in America*. Boston, MA:
    Beacon Press, 1993.

Pollack, Rachel. *The Body of the Goddess*. Shaftesburey, Dorset: Element,
    1997.

The Silappadikaram. Translated by V. R. Ramachanndra Dikshitar,
    Oxford: Oxford University Press, 1939.

Squire, Charles. *Celtic Myth and Legend*. Van Nuys, CA: Newcastle
    Publishing Co., 1975.

Stone, Merlin. *Ancient Mirrors of Womanhood, Volumes 1 and 2*. New York:
    New Sybelline Books, 1979.

Stone, Merlin. *When God Was a Woman*. New York: Dial Press, 1976.

Walker, Barbara G. *The Woman's Encyclopedia of Myths and Secrets*. San
    Francisco CA: Harper and Row, 1983.

Wolkstein, Diana and Samuel Noah Kramer. *Inanna, Queen of Heaven and
    Earth*. New York: Harper and Row, 1983.

And a great Website on dark goddesses:
    http://home.earthlink.net/persepha/DarkGoddess.html

about the author

Trina Robbins has been called Bad by the best of them. More polite people simply refer to her as "outspoken." She has the loudest shout in her self-defense class.

Trina has written about such improper women as Margo St. James, who formed a union for prostitutes, as well as books about superheroines and grrrlz. She has been a pagan since 1977, she can't live without cats, and she considers herself the oldest grrrl in San Francisco.

Books by Trina Robbins

From Girls to Grrrlz

Tomorrow's Heirlooms

The Great Women Superheroes

A Century of Women Cartoonists

Catswalk

Women and the Comics (with Catherine Yronwode)

To Our Readers

Conari Press publishes books on topics ranging from spirituality, personal growth, and relationships to women's issues, parenting, and social issues. Our mission is to publish quality books that will make a difference in people's lives—how we feel about ourselves and how we relate to one another. We value integrity, compassion, and receptivity, both in the books we publish and in the way we do business.

As a member of the community, we sponsor the Random Acts of Kindness™ Foundation, the guiding force behind Random Acts of Kindness™ Week. We donate our damaged books to nonprofit organizations, dedicate a portion of our proceeds from certain books to charitable causes, and continually look for new ways to use natural resources as wisely as possible.

Our readers are our most important resource, and we value your input, suggestions, and ideas about what you would like to see published. Please feel free to contact us, to request our latest book catalog, or to be added to our mailing list.

2550 Ninth Street, Suite 101
Berkeley, California 94710-2551
800-685-9595 • 510-649-7175
fax: 510-649-7190 • e-mail: conari@conari.com
www.conari.com